INSTITUTE OF LEADERSHIP & MANAGEMENT **ilm**

SUPERSERIES

Project and Report Writing

FOURTH EDITION

Published for the
Institute of Leadership & Management by

Pergamon
Flexible
Learning

OXFORD   AMSTERDAM   BOSTON   LONDON   NEW YORK   PARIS
SAN DIEGO   SAN FRANCISCO   SINGAPORE   SYDNEY   TOKYO

Pergamon Flexible Learning
An imprint of Elsevier
Linacre House, Jordan Hill, Oxford OX2 8DP
30 Corporate Drive, Burlington, MA 01803

First published 1986
Second edition 1991
Third edition 1997
Fourth edition 2003
Reprinted 2005, 2006

British Library Cataloguing in Publication Data
A catalogue record for this book is available from the British Library

ISBN 13: 978 0 7506 5876 8
ISBN 10: 0 7506 5876 2

06 07 08 09 10   10 9 8 7 6 5 4 3

For information on Pergamon Flexible Learning
visit our website at www.bh.com/pergamonfl

Institute of Leadership & Management
Registered office
1 Giltspur Street
London
EC1A 9DD
Telephone 020 7294 3053
www.i-l-m.com
ILM is a subsidiary of the City & Guilds Group

Working together to grow
libraries in developing countries

www.elsevier.com | www.bookaid.org | www.sabre.org

ELSEVIER   BOOK AID International   Sabre Foundation

The views expressed in this work are those of the authors and do
not necessarily reflect those of the Institute of Leadership &
Management or of the publisher

Author: Clare Donnelly and Howard Senter
Editor: Clare Donnelly
Editorial management: Genesys, www.genesys-consultants.com
Based on previous material by: Wendy and W. M. Payne, and Howard Senter

Printed and bound in Great Britain

Contents

Contents

Workbook introduction

1 ILM Super Series study links

This workbook addresses the issues of *Project and Report Writing*. Should you wish to extend your study to other Super Series workbooks covering related or different subject areas, you will find a comprehensive list at the back of this book.

2 Links to ILM qualifications

This workbook relates to the following learning outcomes in segments from the ILM Level 3 Introductory Certificate in First Line Management and the Level 3 Certificate in First Line Management.

C2.4 Producing Project Reports
1 Identify objectives and user(s) of the project report
2 Collect information for use in the report
3 Plan the structure of the report according to requirements and guidance
4 Make appropriate use of statistical and visual materials, and appendices
5 Present the report appropriately to stimulate action

3 Links to S/NVQs in Management

This workbook relates to the following elements of the Management Standards which are used in S/NVQs in Management, as well as a range of other S/NVQs.

D1.1   Gather required information
D1.2   Inform and advise others

It will also help you develop the following Personal Competences:

- acting assertively;
- building teams;
- communicating;
- influencing others;
- searching for information;
- thinking and taking decisions.

4 Workbook objectives

Managers are in charge of large amounts of activity, people, money and other resources. In today's 'leaner' and 'flatter' organizations these responsibilities continue to increase.

Managers need to monitor what's going on, and to make decisions, and for this they need information. But there's always too much going on for managers to keep detailed tabs on everything. Information is locked up in record systems, files, archives, documents – and people's memories.

Modern organizations actually produce more information than ever before in history. Computers churn it out in colossal amounts. The trouble is that there's so much information that it's increasingly hard to make sense of it.

Sometimes it seems that the more information there is, the less use it is.

Since managers must have the information, an answer must be found, and one answer is the report. Someone must wade through the piles of information, pick out the important bits, analyse their significance and package it up conveniently.

That's what reports are about. The writer gathers the information, analyses it, selects what's important, works out what it means, and explains it all simply and concisely. If the process of collecting and analysing the information is substantial, you or your organization might term this a 'project', the outcome of which is usually a special report (as it is with an ILM Certificate in First Line Management project). A good report puts the whole of a complex issue 'in a nutshell', and simplifies the task of the decision-makers enormously.

But what is 'a good report'?

If this system is going to work, the person who writes the report must be skilful. He or she must be capable of producing a document that is:

- thorough;
- reliable;
- credible;
- easy for the user to understand.

Those are important skills for anyone in a management role. They help you get on top of information, and you develop the ability to persuade and influence, as well as inform, your colleagues and superiors.

In this workbook we will explain what is required when writing a long document such as a report, proposal, feasibility study, project etc. In doing so, we will provide you with guidelines for planning your work, organizing your activities and collecting information. There are many pitfalls in analysing data, and we will explain some of these.

The workbook will show you how to structure a document, how to write your document simply and clearly, and how to lay it out in a professional manner that will impress your reader. And as you work through the Sessions, we will guide you through the process of creating an actual document and help you produce an ILM Certificate in First Line Management project report.

4.1 Objectives

When you have completed this workbook you will be better able to:

- identify what a report is about and who it is for;
- plan and prepare for writing a report;

- identify and collect the relevant data and information;
- analyse and interpret data correctly;
- adopt a suitable structure for your report;
- write clearly and simply and present your arguments in a fair and unbiased way;
- use tables, diagrams and graphics effectively;
- plan and produce an ILM Certificate in First Line Management project report;
- produce a report that is thorough, reliable, credible and readable.

5 Activity planner

If you are compiling an S/NVQ portfolio, you may like to develop the following Activities as evidence of your competence.

- Activity 3: in which you analyse some routine reports
- Activity 38: which encourages you to practise presenting data in graphical form.

They are marked with the 'Portfolio of evidence' icon shown on the left.

The Work-based assignment is also designed to form the basis of possible acceptable evidence for your portfolio and also to enable you to demonstrate your personal competence in communication and presentation, influencing others and carrying out an information search.

This workbook differs from others in the series in that you will be asked to make a start on the Work-based assignment in Activity 11 and to add to it in Activities 17, 20, 21, 22, 29, 30 and 39. The Work-based assignment asks you to write a report which may also be your ILM project or another quite separate assignment which you are carrying out for your job or as part of your study programme.

You will need to identify a subject for your report and may like to look ahead to these Activities.

You should also note that the main report-writing processes addressed in Sessions A, B and C and developed through the Work-based assignment Activities are also covered in a more concise guide and checklist in Session D. You may wish to refer ahead to this as you develop your project.

Session A
Reports – what and why?

1 Introduction

If you know anything about management, you'll know that there always seem to be lots of reports flying around. They're constantly arriving on people's desks, being discussed, or being requested.

This can seem a bit of a mystery at first. Why bother to grind out all this dull stuff? (A lot of it is rather dull.) Why bother to read it? Why don't we just get on with doing something useful – like our jobs?

Good questions – but there's a good answer.

It's to do with information. The people who run organizations need as much information and knowledge as they can get hold of, because information is the key to success. You can't make good decisions if you don't know what's going on. You can't develop the right products, open branches in the right areas, or invest your money in the right kind of expansion. You don't know what's going wrong, and you are guessing at what is going right.

Without information you may make a good decision once in a while – by sheer chance! But all the important decisions depend on having accurate and reliable information to work on.

Now, modern organizations have access to enormous amounts of information. Their sales, personnel, production and administrative computers produce it by the ton. Much more information comes from outside. The problem is that there's too much. The managers who make the decisions simply don't have the time to digest it all.

That's where reports come in. Someone – like you – will go over the basic facts and figures, and pre-digest them for the benefit of others.

'Knowledge is the business fully as much as the customer is the business ... knowledge is a specifically human resource. It is not found in books. Books contain information, whereas knowledge is the ability to apply information to specific work and human performance. And that only comes with a human being ...'
Peter Drucker (1964), *Managing for Results*, Butterworth-Heinemann.

1

So when you write a report you're playing a vital role for your organization. You're making crucial information available to key people so that important decisions can be made. It's a particularly vital kind of communication.

Reports come in many forms, and we won't try to cover them all, but we will deal with all the important points that they have in common. As you'll see, exactly the same lessons will apply to preparing and writing up your ILM Certificate in First Line Management project report.

2 What is a report?

A report is a summary. It examines a large and/or complex area of information and summarizes all the important issues in a few pages.

There are many kinds of report, as we shall see, but I want to start by thinking about two main types:

■ routine reports, which show how an organization's activities are progressing;
■ special reports, which deal with one-off problems and issues.

2.1 Routine reports

Most organizations are dominated by routine (and some really hate anything that breaks the routine). Departments, branches, workteams and individuals spend their time doing more or less the same things week in and week out.

However, there are always variations.

Routine reports deal with an organization's everyday activities. They are designed to answer questions such as 'What have we done? How much did it cost? How much did we earn?' These financial and activity reports almost always measure actual performance against budgets, targets or forecasts.

The Cramley Healthcare Trust budgeted for 185 varicose vein operations per month. Each month the Surgical Department routinely reported a figure within half a dozen of the budgeted total, that is, between 179 and 191 operations per month. Then in February, the number of varicose vein operations fell suddenly to 33. Immediately the hospital managers wanted to know why.

Activity 1

3 mins

The planned monthly total was 185, but if it sometimes fell to 179 or rose to 191, no one was worried. Why not?

_____

_____

_____

_____

The fall to 33 in February led to an immediate investigation. Why?

_____

_____

_____

_____

The answers are probably quite obvious, but I want to spell them out.

No one worried about small variations against planned totals because:

- they don't have much impact on the Trust's income;
- such variations aren't 'significant' in a statistical sense, because everyone realizes that small hitches can occur: a patient isn't able to come in at the last moment, a surgeon has to break off to deal with an emergency, or other operations are cancelled for some reason, leaving a bit more time on the schedules to deal with varicose veins;
- small variations tend to average out over a period.

A big variation is (or should be) taken more seriously because:

- it can make a big difference to finances – surgeons, theatres, nurses etc. are left doing nothing;
- it implies that something fairly significant has happened.

When the report in question is a routine one, the vast majority of the results will be within the expected range. What managers are looking for are differences that really are significant. These are what need to be explained or highlighted in routine reports, as well as in special reports.

2.2 Quantitative routine reports

An organization may generate dozens of routine management reports.

These are often quantitative in nature – they deal purely with numbers of transactions, or amounts of money, rather than with the nature or quality of what is going on.

Here is an example of an organization where a quantitative routine report gives significant information.

■ **Batchwork Distribution Ltd**

This warehouse and distribution firm stores and delivers stock under contracts with large supermarket chains.

Its routine management reports include:

1   Warehouse
    ■ stock movements inwards (weekly)
    ■ stock movements out (weekly)
    ■ average value of stock held (weekly)
    ■ warehouse staff productivity report (staff hours worked and volume of movements handled) (weekly)
    ■ warehouse overheads (monthly)
    ■ stock losses/wastage (monthly)

2   Office/financial
    ■ size, quantity and value of orders received from supermarkets (weekly)
    ■ payments made and received (daily and weekly)
    ■ office staff productivity report (staff hours worked and transactions undertaken) (weekly)
    ■ errors and returns (weekly)
    ■ office overheads (monthly)

3   Vehicle depot
    ■ activity report: mileage travelled, fuel used, vehicle availability (weekly)
    ■ breakdown/accident/incident report (weekly)
    ■ driver hours/productivity (weekly)
    ■ depot overheads (monthly)

This is far from being a complete list, because the whole of this organization's success depends on its being able to predict and control the figures very finely. Its managers spend many hours poring over reports to ensure that they are:

- meeting customers' needs;
- meeting quality standards;
- achieving the required profit margin.

We can sum up these reports by saying:

- they are all designed to tell managers what we did, how much it cost, and how much we earned;

- they are all designed to reveal differences that are significant.

Here are some figures from Batchwork Distribution Eastern Region's office Activity (Orders Placed) Report.

	March	April	May	June	July	August	September
No of orders received	216	229	244	249	258	275	277
Total value (£)	516044	535076	559228	526444	538788	567540	572341
Cumulative value (£)	516044	1051120	1610348	2136792	2675580	3243120	3815461
Budget (£)	520000	530000	530000	552500	552500	560000	565000
Cumulative budget (£)	520000	1050000	1580000	2132500	2685000	3245000	3810000
Variance (£)	–3956	5076	29228	–26056	–13712	7540	7341
Cumulative variance (£)	–3956	1120	30348	4292	–9420	–1880	5461
Average order size (£)	2389.09	2336.58	2291.92	2114.23	2088.33	2063.78	2066.21

The data show some unsatisfactory trends. The monthly number of orders received is rising faster than the monthly total value of orders. This means that the average value of orders (which is monthly value of orders divided by the monthly number of orders) is decreasing (£2389.09 in March, £2066.21 in September).

Activity 2

5 mins

What does this difference mean for the company in practice? What difference does it make – is it significant?

_____

_____

_____

You will probably agree that it makes quite a big difference: there are 'economies of scale' in the distribution business, for this reason. If you have to send a lorry from a warehouse in, say, Northampton, to deliver an order to, say, Great Yarmouth, the cost in terms of time, fuel and organization is the same if the value of the order is £500 or £5000. But if it is only worth £500, the relative cost of transporting it is much higher. The charge will therefore have to be higher.

Batchwork's costs per £1 of order received are therefore inevitably increasing. This could be bad news for profits.

That was an example of what routine reports can do, and why they are important. Modern organizations are capable of producing masses of such reports quite automatically through their computerized 'transaction processing systems'.

Computerization has transformed the processing of facts and figures, but it takes a human being to extract the useful information from such 'raw' data.

2.3 Routine activity reports

The other common kind of routine report deals less with numbers than with descriptions of things, and information about people's views, attitudes, feelings etc. An obvious example is a regular report on the activity of a team.

This may well include numbers (e.g. 'last month Batchwork's order office B shift team took 261 orders worth ...' etc). But it might well include other kinds of information, for example:

■ **Team Leader's Report**

'February was an unusually busy month, due to the bad weather which:

- increased rates of sickness absence
- resulted in a lot of extra work in rescheduling deliveries held up by bad road conditions
- caused three power failures with some loss of data.'

Regular 'slots' in the team activity report might include:

- people joining/leaving the team;
- details of major problems encountered;
- training undertaken;
- new projects or activities taken on;
- old ones completed;
- secondments, special tasks and additional activities of various kinds;
- suggestions from team members.

Activity 3

S/NVQ D1.1

This Activity may provide the basis of appropriate evidence for your S/NVQ portfolio. If you are intending to take this course of action, it might be better to write your answers on separate sheets of paper.

At this point I suggest that you do some simple analysis on the routine reports that are generated in your department (or in some other part of your organization, provided you have access to both the reports and the data on which they are based).

1   Transfer the following headings onto one or more separate sheets of paper, and add the relevant details.

- Report title
- Who produces the report?
- Frequency (weekly or monthly etc.)
- Content
- Who receives it?
- What they are expected to do with it?

2   Identify as many routine reports as possible and write down the details under these headings.

3   Highlight any routine reports that you personally produce (or contribute to).

4   Summarize briefly what you think these reports contribute to the efficient running of the organization.

If you wish to add this work to your portfolio, include some examples of routine reports you use or to which you contribute.

2.4 Special reports

We've just been looking at the routine reports which all organizations produce, frequently in great numbers.

Regular routine reports have advantages for the people who produce them, because they know:

- what the report is expected to achieve (its objectives);
- what the report is expected to contain;
- how the report should be laid out;
- when the report is needed by;
- roughly how long the report will take to complete.

Such a report also makes life easier for the people who have to read it – its users – because they know:

- when the report will arrive;
- what it will contain;
- whereabouts the interesting bits can be found;
- by whom, when, and on what basis it was produced.

The chances are that none of this will be true for special, one-off reports.

Activity 4 · 5 mins

What sort of situations might call for a one-off report to be written? List **four** or **five** possibilities, preferably drawing on your own experience.

_____

_____

_____

_____

_____

_____

_____

_____

_____

Many one-off reports may relate to 'critical incidents' such as:

- an accident involving (or perhaps caused by) one of the organization's vehicles;
- a fire, flood or power blackout;
- a serious disciplinary incident;
- a security breach (intruders, burglary, major unexplained loss);
- a serious complaint from a customer;
- a major problem of work performance by an individual or a team;
- any incident involving a serious financial loss or marketing failure (e.g. the loss of a major client).

On the other hand, the issue may not be a single 'critical incident' but a situation which has built up, or might be building up, into something more serious:

- the state of the premises;
- error rates in taking customers' orders;
- whether the organization's stationery is old-fashioned and ought to be updated;
- whether the management training scheme is serving its purpose;
- falling productivity in a particular area;
- the state of employee morale;
- the fall-off in demand for a particular product.

The possibilities are literally endless.

Activity 5 · 3 mins

Note down brief details of a 'one-off' special report that has come your way, or that you have been involved in producing. What would you say were the objectives of the report?

Report title and brief detail: **Objectives:**

_____   _____

_____   _____

_____   _____

_____   _____

_____   _____

I can't possibly guess what reports you have named, but I think there are two likely objectives:

Either they were 'for the record', because the law, the system or common sense required details to be put down in writing in case they were needed at some later date. (This would be true of an accident report, for instance, or any incident that might result in an insurance claim or a serious complaint.)

Or they were designed to prompt action and help someone make a decision.

3 Objectives of reports

Whatever the type of report, there is no point producing it unless you want to achieve something – that is, reports need to have a purpose or objective.

In the case of routine reports, we have seen that the objectives are:

■ to provide a record of events;
■ to alert us to variations from what is expected.

In addition, special reports have the objectives of:

■ highlighting critical incidents;
■ drawing attention to changes.

And on top of all that, all reports can have the objectives of:

■ helping people to make decisions;
■ persuading people of something.

3.1 Reports and decisions

Without the right information, it's more or less impossible to make good decisions. Reports are one of the most important ways of feeding information to decision makers; the food is much more easily swallowed if you (or someone) has already made it more digestible.

Activity 6 ·

5 mins

Let's look again at the list of situations covered by special reports that follows Activity 4. Against each one, write down what decisions you think might be based on this report.

a   the state of the premises

_____

b   error rates in taking customers' orders

_____

c   whether the organization's stationery is old-fashioned and ought to be updated

_____

d   whether the company management training scheme is serving its purpose

_____

e   falling productivity in a particular area

_____

f   the state of employee morale

_____

g   the fall-off in demand for a particular product

_____

In all these cases, the questions that the decision maker will ask are these:

■   Is there a real problem?
■   If so, is it big enough to need action?
■   If action is needed, what action?

In other words, he or she is saying 'Do I need to make a decision, and if so, what?'

The person who wrote the report may well have made recommendations, or evaluated various options. If so, that is another helpful bit of pre-digestion!

3.2 Reports and persuasion

Decision makers primarily want the facts – report writers are expected to provide reliable information on which decisions can be based. The writer's personal interpretations – and opinions – are **not** what the report is for.

This isn't always so, if the whole report is designed to persuade others of the writer's case, e.g. it is a 'proposal' document.

Wendy was concerned that the standard of the meals service for elderly people was lower than it should be. She thought there were two main problems: lack of choice in meals, and meals being served inconveniently early or late.

Hearing that another district had a better system, she arranged to visit a contact there. She felt this system had a lot of advantages, so she noted how the meals service was administered, and asked various questions.

When she returned she decided to write a report to the Director of Services.

Activity 7

5 mins

What would you say was the objective of Wendy's report?

_____

_____

Wendy organized her report into four main blocks. If you were in her shoes, what would you expect these blocks to cover?

Block 1: _____

Block 2: _____

Block 3: _____

Block 4: _____

Wendy's objective is obviously to inform, but it goes further than that: she wants to **persuade**. She has identified ways in which the meals service could be improved, and she is putting forward arguments for doing so. I think she would arrange her report to cover the following main topics:

1 an outline of the existing problem as she saw it, with evidence to show that there *was* a problem

2 her explanation of why it was happening

3 a description of how things were done in the other district

4 her proposals for improvements.

Activity 8 · 5 mins

Persuading other people of your case is not usually easy. They have their own ideas and pet schemes, and you may meet resistance.

What could Wendy do to make her report more persuasive?

_____

_____

_____

_____

_____

_____

_____

There are many things that she could do, but most of them should be ruled out. Let's look at some helpful things she could do:

■ First, she can make her arguments as clear and logical as possible.
■ Second, she can support them with facts and figures. What is the level of dissatisfaction? What precisely are the differences between the service in the two districts? What are the cost implications of changing to a different system?
■ Third, she can evaluate any disadvantages of changing the system, and suggest how they can be minimized.

These three things are big pluses. They amount to:

■ clear presentation;
■ thorough consideration of the issues;
■ reliable evidence;
■ logical argument.

Then there are some less creditable things she could do. She could:

■ use dramatic and colourful language to describe the horrors of the present system and the delights of the one she proposes;
■ omit or 'skate over' facts that weaken her case;
■ tamper with the evidence to make it appear more favourable (this does happen, unfortunately);
■ fabricate figures, quotations, case studies (again, this has been known);
■ try to apply moral pressure by making emotive statements such as 'We have a clear duty to rescue our clients from this dire situation';
■ use false or spurious logic in her arguments.

In most kinds of report, the facts and figures are pre-digested to simplify the task of the decision makers who read it, and to make the argument of the report more persuasive. The report must do everything to deserve credibility and confidence.

That means that a report must be:

■ relevant;
■ thorough;
■ reliable;
■ credible;
■ readable.

If it is all of those, it will succeed in communicating the facts and ideas it contains.

We shall see more about how to write a report which has these qualities in later sessions.

In 1991, historian Peter Linebaugh published a controversial book called *The London Hanged*, a study of 1242 people executed for mostly minor crimes in London in the eighteenth century. He was attacked by many other historians for his conclusions. The most damaging attack was from Sir Keith Thomas, who found a handful of errors in Linebaugh's pen-portraits of the individuals concerned. This was used to suggest that Linebaugh was careless with the facts, thus undermining the validity of everything he had to say.

4 The users of reports

So far we have looked at certain types of reports and their objectives, and that one way of thinking about these is: 'what am I trying to achieve in writing this report?'

Another way of looking at it is: 'what is the user of the report trying to achieve in reading this report?' We should take their needs and objectives into account.

Activity 9

5 mins

Lorna Johnson is the sales manager of two divisions of High Wire Productions. It is 5 August and her boss has asked her to explain, at a meeting on 7 August, the sales figures for the first half year to 30 June. She asked her assistant, Miles Collins, to produce a report for her meeting with the boss by 1 August.

Today she received Miles' report. It covers the three months to 30 April, and gives a purely written account of the sales activity in Division A, ignoring Division B. There are no figures at all, and no evidence backing up any of Miles' often extreme assertions about the performance of individual staff members whom he dislikes. It also contains criticisms of the production side of the organization.

What is wrong with Miles' report?

_____

_____

_____

I hope you'll agree that, as far as Lorna is concerned, the report represents very bad quality information.

Generally the users of reports – the decision makers – want information that is of good quality. So the report should:

- relate to the relevant time period (six months to 30 June, not three months in the middle);
- be received at the required time (1 August, not 5 August);
- have an appropriate mix of objectivity and subjectivity (Miles' report is entirely subjective);
- ideally be as quantitative as possible, since for most people numbers are digested more easily (it is not quantitative);
- be accurate (there are no figures or evidence, so its accuracy is unknown);
- be as complete as possible (it only covers Division A);
- not be broader than is necessary (it goes outside sales to look at production);
- have the appropriate level of detail (there is none).

We shall look at an example of a badly written and presented report in Session B, but first we need to think about how we can meet the user's needs and also the objectives of the report itself by making sure that we plan its structure carefully.

Remember that the information and guidance provided in these sessions are for general reports. Specific guidance for your ILM Certificate in First Line Management report is provided in Session D and in the ILM guidance documentation provided by your centre.

5 The structure of a report

All through this workbook we're going to focus on how your report can achieve three broad aims:

- to make your reader's task easier;
- to communicate your messages and ideas more effectively;
- to maximize credibility.

Structure has got a lot to do with this. Planning and presenting a report with a good structure definitely helps the reader (it helps the writer too, as a matter of fact); it also helps your credibility to use a 'professional' structure.

It's realistic to talk about 'a professional structure' because there are professionals out there who write reports for a living – consultants of various kinds, for example. In addition, you may be required to produce a report in a standard format, and often these will be of the type used by consultants.

This is how a consultant would usually structure a report:

1 Title page

2 Contents list

3 Objective/terms of reference

4 Summary

5 Introduction

6 Main body of the report

7 Conclusions

8 Recommendations

9 Appendices

I'll take you briefly through these one by one now. We shall see more about each of them in later sessions.

5.1 Title page

This will usually feature:

- the **title** (and often a **subtitle** too);
- the name of person or organization to whom the report is addressed;
- the name of the writers (and the organization for which they work, if appropriate);
- the date of submission of the report.

Often report writers use very dull titles like 'Report of an investigation into the better utilization of floorspace in Workshop C'. This may be absolutely accurate, but more can be done with titles. For example, it will be a small, but real, help to effective communication if the title is **eye-catching** and **memorable** as well as **informative**. For example, a report on (lack of) progress in improving disabled access to Council properties could be entitled:

Disappointed Hopes

A review of progress in improving disabled access to Council properties

---

Activity 10

5 mins

Go back to the case study about Wendy and the meals service in Activities 7 and 8. Could you suggest **two** or **three** alternatives for an eye-catching, memorable and informative title? (You will probably want to include a subtitle.)

_____

_____

_____

_____

_____

_____

There are countless possibilities. How about:

> Improving the Meals Service for Elderly People
>
> Into the era of choice and quality

or

> The Meals Service for Elderly People
>
> Five practical proposals for improvement

Just a catch-phrase like 'into the era of choice and quality' will be enough to make the title memorable.

5.2 A list of contents

This won't be necessary for a very short report, but it helps readers 'take in' the structure of the report at a glance.

5.3 Objectives and terms of reference

Objectives are aims and goals described in detail. In Wendy's case, she probably drew up her primary aims and her objectives like this:

■ Aim:

  ■ to show how the meals service for elderly people could be improved.

■ Objectives:

  ■ to identify those aspects of the meals service that users find unsatisfactory;
  ■ to compare the service provided in our district with that provided in B_____ district;
  ■ to suggest what specific improvements could be made in our service;
  ■ to evaluate the cost and other implications of implementing them.

As you can see, the report's objectives are the **specific things that have to be done** in order to achieve the report's primary aim.

Terms of Reference (which I'll refer to as TORs) are not quite the same as objectives. They are a way of **defining the subject and scope of a report or project**.

You may have heard of TORs in relation to official investigations and Committees of Inquiry (such as the Macpherson Inquiry into the death of Stephen Lawrence) or to research projects.

A job description could be called the TORs of one's employment. From another angle, TORs can be seen as authority to investigate certain matters.

5.4 Summary

This is sometimes called an 'executive summary'. It describes the content and conclusions of the report briefly (usually in around 150–500 words). It does not normally include data or other evidence – this is all in the main report.

The Summary will always include the writers' main conclusions; it will often include their principal recommendations.

5.5 Introduction

Here is a checklist of what an introduction typically contains:

- when and by whom the report was commissioned;
- what purpose it is expected to serve;
- the terms of reference and specific objectives;
- how the writers went about preparing it (what data they used, what research they did, who they spoke to etc.);
- the methods they used for analysing their data, if appropriate (this would be important for market research reports, among others);
- what problems they encountered, and how they dealt with them;
- what steps they took to consult with their clients;

There may be other information in the introduction, depending on the nature of the report.

When you are writing a report or project, you won't need to deal with all of these points; on the other hand it might be useful to include a schedule describing the research and investigation work that you undertook (but only if it's likely to impress!)

5.6 The main body of the report

The main body of the report is the detailed description of what the writers discovered, what it means and how important it is: **facts**, **analysis** and **evaluation**, to put it in technical terms. It will contain evidence for its findings, in the shape of quantitative data. These will often be shown as simple tables, graphs and charts.

It's not a good idea to load too much data into the report itself, because this hampers effective communication. It's much better to use summary tables and graphs, and put the 'heavy' data into an appendix.

The main report must be broken down into manageable chunks, using numbered headings and subheadings. If the report is long and complex, it may be best to divide it into 'chapters'.

5.7 Conclusions

These sum up in reasonable detail what the report has found. They deal with the facts, and what they mean. The Conclusions section will be longer than the Summary at the beginning of the report, because: it must not only say **what** the writers' conclusions are, but must explain **why** they were reached.

5.8 Recommendations

This section won't always be necessary: sometimes the writer isn't asked to suggest recommendations, only to report the facts. If you decide, or are asked, to include recommendations in a report, don't include too many. Half a dozen is plenty: more, and you may start to confuse people and blur the issues.

5.9 Appendices

A lot of the evidence on which the report was based (especially data, questionnaire results, reports of case studies as well as lists and forms that were relevant to the conduct of the report) should be tacked onto the end as Appendices. Then the reader isn't obliged to plough through this less interesting stuff, but can consult the appendices if he or she wishes.

Note that the structure of the report is strictly logical: it has a beginning, a middle and an end. It begins by explaining what it is, goes on to describe what it found, then ends with the conclusions you draw from the facts. You include what's relevant to the argument, and you push 'background' material into appendices.

6 Types of report

As well as reports, there are lots of other documents to which we can apply the same ideas and approaches. Here are just a few of them.

Jeremy was asked to prepare a **proposal** for offering the charity's advice and information services via the Internet.

_____

Manos was part of a team that prepared a **feasibility study** for transferring the company's manufacturing base from a London suburb to a new location in the Midlands.

_____

Sandra and Gill sat down to draft out an **information handout** describing the library's facilities and how other staff could get the most from them.

_____

Pete drew up the 'Best Practice' **guidelines** for dealing with patients under the age of 18.

_____

Raisa drafted out a **guide to the organization** which was given to people applying for jobs.

_____

Janice developed an extensive **specification document** giving would-be suppliers guidance in preparing and submitting their tenders.

_____

Many of you will be involved in preparing such documents in years to come. For those of you pursuing an ILM programme, the biggest opportunity to apply your report-writing skills will be in preparing your ILM Certificate project report.

Activity 11

15 mins

S/NVQ D1.1, D1.2

This Activity may provide the basis of appropriate evidence for your S/NVQ portfolio. If you are intending to take this course of action, it might be better to write your answers on separate sheets of paper.

Work-based assignment

Your Work-based assignment doubles as a Workbook assessment. The aim of the Assignment is to plan, prepare and write a report. You will find out more about this as we go along, but first you will need to choose a subject.

The guidelines for choosing a subject are these:

1   The subject must be a **management** issue, not a **technical** one. So 'planning and implementing the introduction of a new computer system' would be acceptable, but 'designing a new computer programme' would not. It must focus on **management** rather than operational problems.

2   The report must involve you in:

   a   **investigating** an issue or problem of some kind
   b   **researching** to find or produce data (facts)
   c   **analysing** those facts to draw out **logical conclusions and recommendations**
   d   **presenting** the facts, analysis, conclusions and recommendations in **a professional manner**
   e   supporting your text with **tables**, **graphics** and **spreadsheets**.
   f   **producing** a smart and well-laid-out 'hard copy' of the report.

Spend some time deciding the subject for your report. You will need to discuss it with your manager, and colleagues may have helpful suggestions too.

When you have decided on a subject, write brief details down here, as well as on the separate sheets of paper that you will be using for the assignment itself:

_____

_____

_____

From now on you should be collecting information and ideas relevant to this report whenever you can.

Self-assessment 1

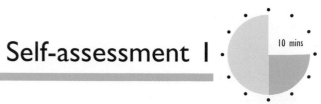

1   Complete these statements so that they make sense:

   a   A report examines an area of information and _____ all the important issues.

   b   Many routine reports are designed to reveal the _____ that make a real _____.

   c   The role of a management report is to pre- _____ information for _____ makers.

   d   A report, to be useful, should feature:

   ■   clear _____;

   ■   thorough _____ of the issues;

   ■   reliable _____;

   ■   _____ argument.

2   Explain briefly why regular, routine reports are fairly straightforward to produce.

   _____

   _____

   _____

   _____

3   Give **three** examples of the kind of reports that might be needed 'for the record'.

   _____

   _____

   _____

4   In order to successfully communicate the facts and ideas it contains, a report must be: r_____, th_____, r_____, c_____ and r_____.

5   List the standard features of a report's structure.

   Answers to these questions can be found on page 115.

7 Summary

- Reports play a key role in pre-digesting information so that decision makers can use it effectively. They examine a large and/or complex area of information and summarize all the important issues in a few pages.

- Routine reports are usually straightforward to produce, because they follow a regular pattern; an organization may generate scores of them. They are designed to tell managers:
  - what we did;
  - how much it cost;
  - how much we earned, etc.;

  and to reveal significant variations.

- Special reports are one-offs, and are generally longer and harder to produce.

  They may relate to 'critical incidents', to situations that are perhaps developing into something more serious; or to future prospects.

  Their purpose is usually to enable decision makers:
  - to decide whether there is a problem or an opportunity;
  - if so, whether it is big enough to call for action;
  - and what action this should be.

- The standard structure of a report requires the following elements:
  - title page;
  - contents list;
  - objectives/terms of reference;
  - summary;
  - introduction;
  - main body;
  - conclusions;
  - recommendations;
  - appendices.

- The principles that apply to management reports also apply to other longer documents, such as:
  - proposals;
  - feasibility studies;
  - information handouts;
  - guidelines;
  - organization guides;
  - specification documents;
  - ILM Certificate in First Line Management projects.

- Terms of Reference are often set for reports (and always are for ILM projects). They may include objectives, but their main role is to define the subject and scope of the report, that is, its focus in space and time, i.e.:
  - what areas, activities and people should be covered;
  - over what period of time they should be examined;
  - what the deadline for completion is;
  - what matters should be excluded.

Session B
The report writing process

1 Introduction

If it's going to achieve its specific objectives, and meet the objectives of its users, a report or a project must be:

■ relevant;
■ thorough;
■ reliable;
■ credible;
■ readable.

A lot may ride on the result – the quality of important decisions, the fate of your pet projects, your own reputation.

As we discussed in Session A, with routine reports the task is fairly simple. Models of what's required already exist, and the collection, analysis and presentation of facts is also routine. You will present the report in a routine format.

With special reports, ILM Certificate in First Line Management projects and other longer written documents, the task is different:

■ the issues will often be complex;
■ the facts and figures won't be presented on a plate: you'll have to go out and find them;
■ you won't necessarily know what the end result will be;
■ you may not have standard formats to work to;
■ the length and detail of the report will depend on the subject, and what you find when you start examining it.

All in all, you will need to make a big investment of time, energy and brainpower.

You need to get it right, and the key to doing so is careful planning and thorough preparation.

You may be used to writing documents, such as letters and memos, for other people. How different can report writing be?

Let's see first how it can all go wrong!

2 What's special about presenting reports?

There are several big differences between writing a short document like a memo and writing a proper report.

> Jamail was asked by the committee to write a report on the progress made in installing wheelchair/pushchair access at the County Council's many premises.
>
> He was very busy and was very slow to get started. When he realized how close his deadline was, he hastily phoned some local councillors and community activists. The report he submitted was mainly based on their comments. Beryl Wallace told him 'I hear that the old swimming pool in B_____ still hasn't got a proper ramp, and as for the Youth House, people are always moaning about it.' These 'facts' went into the report.
>
> Jamail's 'final' report was very short – just under two pages. The main body of his report went as follows:

> The Council Equal Opportunities committee passed a resolution some time ago calling for wheelchair/pushchair access to Council premises to be improved. The intention was to see ramps installed at entrances and similar improvements. The cost of these was expected to be considerable.
>
> In the event most of the improvements have not been carried out. This is no doubt due to lack of funds, but also to blame, no doubt, is the lack of enthusiasm on the part

of Council staff. Attitudes towards disabled people are still very poor. This matter has simply not been given the right degree of implementation, or more would have been done. The old swimming pool at B_____ is a case in point. It should have been given a ramp, and this has not happened. Also numerous complaints have been received about the Youth House.

The Assembly Rooms in my own Ward have been improved greatly, but the same cannot be said of elsewhere. Of the other main Council premises there is little good reported.

Yet there is no doubt that improvements are desperately needed and that such improvements would greatly benefit the disabled members of the community, their families and carers. Members of this Committee are united in their belief that this will be a significant step forward in provision for a group that has traditionally been underprivileged. It also conforms with both existing Equal Opportunities policy and the spirit and letter of the 1995 Disablement Discrimination Act.

In general I believe that the policy has failed, and that this is a serious matter for the Council. I recommend that we review performance in this field with care and put forward proposals for action.

Activity 12 · 10 mins

Read through that report again, if you can bear to. What, if anything, would you say is wrong with it as a report?

_____

_____

_____

_____

_____

_____

I'm sure you saw quite a lot that was wrong with Jamail's production.

For a start, there is no structure at all – it's just a series of ideas. Then we already know that he didn't do any proper research, but relied on informal comments from his personal contacts. You probably noticed that he has turned what Beryl Wallace told him about the old swimming pool and the Youth House, which was not only hearsay but second-hand, into fact.

You no doubt noticed the lack of any figures, yet he could usefully have stated:

- the expected cost of the improvements;
- how much was budgeted for them;
- how much of the budget was spent;
- how much work had been done;
- what and where improvements had been made;
- what improvements remained to be made, and where.

Jamail doesn't even say when the relevant resolution was passed (he says 'some time ago').

There is also a good deal of 'waffle' that doesn't contribute anything of importance at all. The fourth paragraph is an obvious example.

Jamail makes value judgements for which he provides scarcely any evidence. He seems very keen to pin the blame on 'lack of enthusiasm on the part of Council staff' and their 'attitudes towards disabled people' which he says – without quoting any evidence – 'are still very poor'.

Let's face it: this is a dreadful 'report'. Here's what the committee chairperson wrote on it:

The Council Equal Opportunities committee passed a resolution some time ago *When?* calling for wheelchair/pushchair access to Council premises to be improved. The intention was to see ramps installed at entrances and similar improvements. The cost of these was expected to be considerable. *How much?*

In the event most *Meaning?* of the improvements have not been carried out. This is no doubt due to lack of funds, but also to blame, no doubt, *If there's no doubt about it where's the evidence?* is the lack of enthusiasm on the part of Council staff. Attitudes towards disabled people are still very poor. *Possibly, but so what?* This matter has simply not been given the right degree of implementation, or more would have been done. *Evidence? None!* The old swimming pool at B_____ is a case in point. It should have been given a ramp, and this has not happened. *Rubbish! I know for a fact this was done — it's the disabled toilets that were never completed?* Also numerous complaints have been received about the Youth House. *Evidence?*

The Assembly Rooms in my own Ward *Presumably Jamail found time to stroll round there and see for himself?* have been improved greatly, but the same cannot be said of elsewhere. *He hasn't checked, has he?* Of the other main Council premises there is little good reported. *Who's he asked?*

Yet there is no doubt that improvements are desperately needed and that such improvements would greatly benefit the disabled members of the community, their families and carers. Members of this Committee are united in their belief that this will be a significant step forward in provision for a group that has traditionally been underprivileged. It also conforms with both existing Equal Opportunities policy and the spirit and letter of the 1995 Disablement Discrimination Act. *Sounds nice — contributes precisely nothing. I don't think this 'Act' exists, at least not under this name.*

In general I believe that the policy has failed, and that this is a serious matter *If it were true it would be serious. I agree!* for the Council. I recommend that we review performance in this field with care and put forward proposals for action. *That's exactly what J. was supposed to do!*

Dreadful report — completely useless!

What this example demonstrates is that, to be useful, a report must be based on accurate and reliable data. Where data are explained and interpreted this must be done in an unbiased way. Above all, it must address and answer the questions that the people who receive it are asking, and it must do so in a clear, logical and well-structured way.

Here is an example of spurious logic from Jamail's 'report':

'This matter has simply not been given the right degree of implementation, or more would have been done.'

This sounds quite serious, but if you look closely all Jamail has actually said is that the work has not been done because it has not been done — a meaningless statement.

Activity 13 · 5 mins

It is very risky to use such manipulative and dishonest tactics to persuade someone of your case. Put yourself in the position of a group of people reading such a report. What might your reaction be?

_____

_____

_____

_____

People who are used to reading and evaluating reports are very sensitive to:

■ emotional language;

■ opinions masquerading as facts;

■ arguments that are not supported by evidence.

You can be absolutely certain that if you write in such a way, you will be challenged.

It's also risky to falsify, hide or tamper with the facts.

Of course, if you submit a report on a metallurgical process to a group of football coaches, you might be able to gamble on getting away with almost any kind of nonsense. But usually, your report will be going to people who have at least some expertise in the subject.

And then someone is bound to spot an error, omission or deliberate distortion: and one will be enough. If it can be shown that one important fact or conclusion is invalid, your report will be fatally undermined.

Reports – special reports in particular – demand time and concentration. And the writer may need to probe deeply into facts, events, processes and motivations hitherto unrevealed. This alone reveals a big difference between 'small-scale' writing and writing reports.

Let's summarize where Jamail went wrong:

1 Focus: He doesn't really state his aim, so his report seems unfocused.

2 Planning: He left it too late to do any proper research and did not leave himself enough time to write a properly structured report.

3   Research: Instead of drafting proper objectives and terms of reference which would have made it clear that a certain amount of information was needed, he simply called up a few people.

4   Structure: There is none.

5   Content: The lack of research and structure means that the report is very short and totally insubstantial. It has no specific conclusions and its one recommendation is really that a proper report should be done!

6   Language: Jamail's language is repetitive, subjective and emotive.

I hope you can see that, to bring all these elements together and produce the report at the end of it involves organization of the report writing process.

3 The report writer's toolkit

First things first – make sure that you have things to hand that you will need, and that you have space to store your materials over the time it takes to go through the process.

■   For writing and making notes you will need:

  ■ pens – two different colours would be useful;
  ■ a pencil and eraser;
  ■ highlighters – again, two different colours.

■   For writing your notes in:

  ■ a small notepad, notebook or a few index cards – keep these with you so you can jot down ideas when they occur;
  ■ Post-it notes – use these to mark passages in documents and books and to write reminders and short notes to yourself;
  ■ a pad of A4 lined paper – use this for drafting out your ideas.

Some people are very keen on using index cards for collecting and organizing ideas and facts. Being postcard-sized, these are handy to use, and they can be shuffled into a different order as your ideas develop. If you use index cards, you will probably want to have a special card box to keep them in.

- For storing your notes and materials in:

  - a ring binder (sheets from your A4 pad will probably have holes punched already), or
  - a sturdy box file – this will be bulky, but the advantage is that you can keep things like pens, index cards and Post-it notes in it as well as papers;
  - storage alternatives include: a wallet-type expandable cardboard file; a large 'job-bag' envelope; a spare briefcase.

  If you are mainly desk-based, you may opt for a special file tray, a spare drawer or a 'slot' in a filing cabinet drawer.

- Other equipment you may need:

  - a calculator;
  - a ruler;
  - squared paper;
  - graph paper;
  - 'analysis paper' (the sort that has columns for writing in figures);
  - a stapler;
  - paperclips;
  - a hole-punch.

If you have access to a computer then you may wish to use this. The word-processing functions of a computer make drafting and correcting reports a great deal easier. Automatic spell-checking can also be a great help.

With a computer you can also do a great deal in terms of:

- laying out your document attractively;
- creating tables and doing complex calculations using a spreadsheet;
- generating graphs and charts from tables (another spreadsheet function);
- creating other kinds of diagrams and illustrations;
- creating 'databases' of information and ideas (the sort of thing that people use hand-written index cards for).

How much you can get from a computer depends on what software is available and how skilful you are in using it. If you don't have access to a computer, don't worry: it may take a little longer, but the report you produce can be of excellent quality whether you have the latest tools or not.

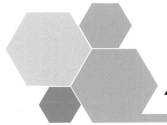

4 Get the task into focus

To focus on something is to concentrate.

If you are asked to produce a report on a clearly defined area then you know what it is that you have to focus on, But what if, like Wendy in Session A, someone were just to say: 'I think there are problems with the service, can you do a report?' Where would you start?

> When Wendy was considering the project she actually started out with a very broad focus – 'problems with the service'.
>
> The grumbles were about several different aspects of the service: the quality of the food, the way it was presented, the behaviour of the staff, the temperature (it was sometimes cold), the lack of variety, the lack of ethnic and vegetarian options, and problems of waste disposal, as well as the issues of choice and serving times.
>
> Wendy thought about producing a strong condemnation of the whole service, but an experienced colleague advised her against this. 'Concentrate on a couple of aspects that are really important', she told Wendy. 'That way you'll reduce the amount of work you're taking on, and you'll get a better result. The best plan is to focus on two or three issues that will really make a difference.'

That's how Wendy came to focus on just two issues: choice and serving times.

She also thought about how she would research into what was happening in other districts. She considered doing a questionnaire-based survey of a sample of districts around the country. Again her colleague had good advice: 'Don't bother with all that. You'll only waste a lot of time and effort. Just go and see what they're doing in B_____. Tino Bassano runs the unit and I know they made a lot of improvements last year. Why don't I arrange for you to go over there and talk to him?'

By focusing in like this, Wendy was able to narrow the scope of the work she would have to do. This saved her a lot of time and also helped her produce a more effective report. You won't always find things quite this easy, though. Often you may need to do a considerable amount of research before you can even frame your aim, objectives and terms of reference.

4.1 Determine the report's general aim and objectives

The aim and objectives of a report are broad and general indications of what it is expected to achieve. They are usually set by whoever commissions the report.

Activity 14   5 mins

Think about Jamail's report, and Wendy's report (which we have just been talking about). What would you say were the aims of these reports?

Jamail's:

_____

_____

_____

Wendy's:

_____

_____

_____

In Jamail's case, the aim was to establish how much had been done to improve disabled access to Council premises.

In Wendy's it was to show how the meals service for elderly people could be improved.

Note that aims don't generally go into much detail: they're a short and broad summary that's easy to focus on. As we saw in Session A, the aim can be broken down further into specific objectives.

4.2 Determine the writer's objectives

Note that so far we have looked at the aims **set for the report**. They are not necessarily the same as the **writer's personal aims**. Wendy, clearly, is motivated by a strong personal desire to achieve a better service for the old people in her care. Jamail, while apparently passionate about disabled access, just wanted to get the report done.

Activity 15 · 5 mins

What goes through your mind when you're asked to write a report? What are your personal objectives in doing so?

_____

_____

_____

_____

_____

_____

_____

_____

If you're like Jamail, your goal might be to perform a burdensome task as quickly as possible, with a minimum investment of time and effort.

However, I think that most of us would say something like:

■ to carry out my duties as required;
■ to make a useful contribution to the organization's work;
■ to develop my own knowledge, skills and understanding;
■ to give a good impression to my colleagues and superiors.

These objectives, may or may not be worthy and useful. The point, however, is that you can only do a professional job by concentrating on the aim and objectives that have been set **for the report itself**, and developing them into terms of reference (TORs).

4.3 Define the terms of reference (TORs)

The TORs define the focus of the work: what is to be included and what is not. The TORs for a report or project authorize you:

to look into a certain matter, within certain parameters (or limits), for a specified purpose.

In practice, the TORs may include the objectives.

The whole idea of the TORs is to give you a clear focus for your work, so they must not be vague.

Something like 'To look into absenteeism' is far too sweeping to be useful.

■ Whose absenteeism? Every employee, from part-time cleaners to the Board of Directors?
■ Absenteeism over what period? Since the firm began in 1831?

TORs must be more definite: 'To analyse absenteeism among counter staff during the last 12 months' would explain the scope and focus of the project quite clearly. However, the TORs should also tell us the aims and objectives of the report, as in the following example.

As part of her management development programme, Cherie was asked:

1 To investigate production hold-ups due to component shortages during the last 12 months.

2 To examine current procedures for replacing component stocks.

3 To evaluate at least two alternative solutions to the identified problems, including a possible change to a just-in-time replenishment system.

4 To recommend the most practical solution within the constraints that exist.

Activity 16 ·

10 mins

Imagine that you are to write a report on 'Car Parking on Company Premises'. You have established that this means all vehicles using any of the designated car parking spaces (i.e. company vehicles and those of employees, visitors and VIPs).

You are expected to come up with ideas for alleviating present complaints: from visitors that they can find nowhere to park; from employees that there is haphazard parking which wastes space, is dangerous, blocks access, etc. You are also to look to future needs (a three-year span is suggested).

Try your hand at writing your TORs.

_____

_____

_____

_____

_____

_____

How did you get on? I didn't find it all that easy, but this is what I came up with:

- to investigate the present usage of parking space (who uses it, when and why?) and identify any problems;
- to forecast the likely parking requirements for the next three years;
- to make recommendations which will improve the present situation and cope with estimated needs for the next three years.

Practise writing TORs for a variety of other reports. Include some that other people are going to write, and see how your own TORs compare.

We can sum up aims, objectives and TORs like this:

- aims and goals are what the report is expected to achieve, in broad general terms;
- objectives are the detailed description of what you need to achieve in order to fulfil the aims and goals;
- Terms of Reference (TORs) lay down the framework and limits in space and time within which you will work;
- aims and objectives are often intermingled, as are objectives and TORs.

Every time you work on your report, go back and read your TORs. This will help you stay on track.

Activity 17 · 12 mins

S/NVQ D1.2

This Activity may provide the basis of appropriate evidence for your S/NVQ portfolio. If you are intending to take this course of action, it might be better to write your answers on separate sheets of paper.

Work-based assignment

Think about the report you selected in Activity 11, and write down:

a the broad aim
b the TORs (including specific objectives).

You may also like to note – elsewhere – your personal aims in undertaking this assignment.

4.4 Establish the parameters

In the TORs, remember to set the parameters.

■ The boundaries in terms of space or things

For instance, are you to look at:

- one department (office, ward, section) or several departments?
- one product or a number of products?
- one type of activity or all types?
- one make of machine or alternative makes?

Are there any no-go areas? Some information might be restricted to certain people. There might be sensitive issues that an organization does not consider appropriate for a relatively junior manager to get involved in. So make sure you know where the 'No Trespassers' signs are!

■ The limits in terms of time

- How far back should the investigation go?
- What is an adequate period to survey?
- When is the final written report due?

5 Plan your work

When you've got a non-routine report, project, or similar long document to produce, you need to plan. Time spent on planning can save many wasted hours and much useless effort. The plan should help you assess:

- how much work it will involve;
- how much time it will take (and how much time you have available);
- what resources you will need.

Most managers do their planning and writing on a personal computer (PC). They may even have planning and project management software available. In many ways this is ideal, but I'm going to assume that you will not be using a computer, as this helps to draw out all the steps in the process. (But if you have access to a PC, by all means use it!)

5.1 Focus on your deadline

Find out what the deadline for submitting the final document is.

Write it in large letters in a bright colour on a large piece of paper. Pin the paper up where you can't help seeing it.

Remember, time is already passing . . .

Your deadline is some time in the future – perhaps quite a long time off. But time flies, and if you don't have a plan, you'll soon find yourself in the same position as Jamail: the deadline's on top of you, and you haven't done a thing.

Bear in mind too that most management reports have tight deadlines. Management culture is about speed, urgency and busy schedules. The pressure will be on from day one.

5.2 Identify the major stages in the report writing process

Let's go back to Jamail again, and the report about progress in improving disabled access to Council premises, which he made such a mess of.

Activity 18 · 5 mins

Put yourself in Jamail's shoes. You've been given your objectives and TORs.

Now, what precisely are you going to have to do in order to deliver a reasonably good report in time for the deadline? Jot down the main stages that occur to you.

_____

_____

_____

_____

_____

You've already got the aims, objectives and TORs, so you are focused and should have a pretty good idea of what to do next.

First you'll also need to allocate time to uncovering the facts. In Jamail's case, this could mean consulting records, checking budgets and audit reports of expenditure, talking with Councillors and Council staff, writing to or telephoning the premises concerned, and probably visiting several of them.

Actually, there could be an enormous amount of activity here, and you would need to think hard about how to reduce the burden of work without unduly affecting the reliability of the report. Don't forget, your job in these situations is to pre-digest the information for other people. It's not to write a complete history of the matter.

After that you will be focusing on the physical report itself.

We can summarize the 'main stages' of preparing a report or project like this.

a   producing a rough workplan

b   thinking about the detail of your investigations

c   carrying out your investigations

d   sorting, sifting and analysing your findings

e   writing a first draft

f   checking and revising your draft

g   refining the layout, adding visuals etc.

h   producing the final version.

It's wise to prepare your workplan in two stages: first an outline, and then, when you've kicked this around a bit, the final version.

Activity 19 · 10 mins

Here's an outline that could apply to many management reports. In this case it refers to a feasibility study on subcontracting the organization's data processing activities to a specialist 'facilities' company.

The deadline for the report is in eight weeks' time (eight days would be more typical of a lot of management reports), which amounts to 40 working days.

I've put the main stages down in the order I think is appropriate. Go over it and allocate time to each stage, by marking in what day you think that activity should start on. We're working backwards from the deadline, so Day 0 is submission day, and Day 40 is start day.

Stage/activity	Day
1 Receive TOR and objectives	40
2 Draft work plan for report	___
3 Identify suitable subcontractors	___
4 Draw up full description of existing DP activities	___
5 Establish costs of existing DP activities	___
6 Hold initial discussions with suitable subcontractors	___
7 Visit most likely contenders to examine how they operate	___
8 Get initial estimates of cost	___
9 Draft out report	___
10 Check and revise first draft	___
11 Prepare and print out final version	___
12 Submit final report	0

Unless you've had some experience of such projects, it is hard to judge the timescales that might be involved in these various activities, but I have a few words of advice.

- Some activities will always take a lot more time than others, so if you've given all the stages equal time that is certainly a mistake.
- Don't underestimate the amount of thinking time needed for processes like identifying suitable subcontractors.
- Don't underestimate how long it can take to contact people, arrange meetings, extract information and estimates from them, and chase up any queries.
- Allow some 'float time' here and there – an extra margin of time in case things don't go quite as smoothly as you expect (they seldom will!).
- Always allow a bit of extra time before Day Zero: in my experience, if you leave production of the final report until the last minute, one of three things will happen (if you are working on a computer):

  - the printer will break down;
  - the computer files will become corrupted, and you'll have to retype part of the material;
  - you'll discover errors you'd overlooked.

5.3 Prepare a detailed action plan

If your report or project is complex, the next stage is to break down your major stages into specific activities, and to list these. This will produce an Action Plan that shows:

- what needs to be done;
- by whom;
- and when.

Here's an extract from an action plan drawn up by a team leader called Sian. The activities will be shared by Sian and her colleague Toni. The last column, as you can see, is for ticking as you complete activities.

	DP Sub-contracting Feasibility Study Stage 3 Identifying suitable subcontractors		**Action Plan**	
Element	**Activity**	**Who?**	**By?**	**OK?**
3.1	Consult colleagues (RM & GG)	Sian	day 39	
3.2	Check list of approved suppliers	Toni	day 39	
3.3	Draw up criteria for suitability	Sian	day 39	
3.4	Contact suppliers informally to assess whether they can meet criteria	Toni	day 38	
3.5	Draw up shortlist	Sian/Toni	day 38	
3.6	Draft formal letter to shortlisted suppliers	Sian	day 37	

If you've ever studied Critical Path Analysis and similar planning techniques you will realize that it's advisable to draw up diagrams showing how these activities interlock, because:

■ some activities must be completed before others can be started (e.g. potential suppliers must be identified before they can be contacted);

■ some activities can go in parallel (e.g. identifying suppliers and drawing up descriptions of the existing operation): in this case, two people are working on the project, so obviously at least some of the tasks can be performed at the same time.

Activity 20

8 mins

S/NVQ D1.1

Work-based assignment

This Activity may provide the basis of appropriate evidence for your S/NVQ portfolio. If you are intending to take this course of action, it might be better to write your answers on separate sheets of paper.

Make a first draft of an action plan for the report you are preparing.

5.4 Use your brain

Some aspects of the report are going to call for thinking, for example:

- what investigations to carry out;
- what the data mean;
- what conclusions you can draw;
- what recommendations are justified;
- what other implications they have.

Here are some hints that you might find useful.

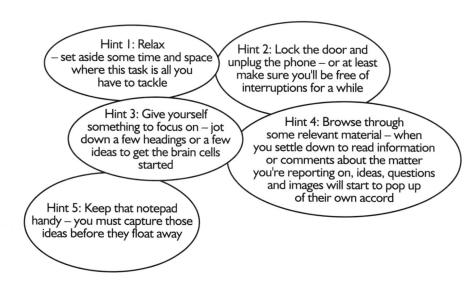

Hint 1: Relax – set aside some time and space where this task is all you have to tackle

Hint 2: Lock the door and unplug the phone – or at least make sure you'll be free of interruptions for a while

Hint 3: Give yourself something to focus on – jot down a few headings or a few ideas to get the brain cells started

Hint 4: Browse through some relevant material – when you settle down to read information or comments about the matter you're reporting on, ideas, questions and images will start to pop up of their own accord

Hint 5: Keep that notepad handy – you must capture those ideas before they float away

Turn your thoughts into a rough list of what you need to do. Consider each item and add notes for yourself on:

EXTENSION 1
At this stage you might like to turn to page 113 of this workbook, where you will find some ideas about ways of researching.

- **what** additional information you might need;
- **where** you might find it;
- **how** you can obtain it;
- **who** might be of help in locating it;
- **who** might be able to provide information.

This can feed into your action plan.

You will soon realize that some things on your list aren't worth bothering about. And the rest will have varying degrees of urgency.

- Why not use symbols (letters, numbers, stars or coloured spots) to indicate your priorities?
- Sort everything you have to do into priority order.
- Ditch the items at the bottom of your list of priorities.
- Rewrite rough lists if they get hard to read.

If you have decided that index cards would suit your way of working, this is when you set them up. Give a reference number to your sheets or cards, then you can make cross-references where something on one sheet is related to, or even depends on, the outcome of another task.

Ultimately you should have a series of pages or cards, each with an idea on it, together with notes of:

- what you need to do;
- where you have to go;
- who must be approached;
- priority rating.

By now you should be in a position to have another go at your action plan.

Activity 21

S/NVQ D1.1

Work-based assignment

This Activity may provide the basis of appropriate evidence for your S/NVQ portfolio. If you are intending to take this course of action, it might be better to write your answers on separate sheets of paper.

At this point go back to your action plan, perhaps after discussing it with colleagues. Now's the time to revise it and draw up a final version in the light of the extra thinking you have done.

6 Research and analyse the facts

The basis of any report must be facts, and not:

■ what you think it might or should have been;
■ what you'd prefer it to be;
■ or what you imagine it probably is.

In carrying out your project, you must put aside your personal feelings. It's best to adopt a 'neutral', and 'scientific' approach. Approach the situation as if it had nothing to do with you personally. Even if you have inside knowledge, remain outside the situation. Above all, shut your prejudices out.

We shall look at this in detail in Session C, along with analysis and presentation.

7 Select the appropriate structure

We saw in Session A that most reports are structured in a fairly standard way. This structure is designed to make both the writer's job – writing the report – and the user's job – reading and acting on the report – easier. We include:

■ title page;
■ contents list (this will be written last);
■ objectives/terms of reference;
■ summary (including conclusions and recommendations);
■ introduction;
■ main body;
■ conclusions;
■ recommendations;
■ appendices.

The standard structure is one that has been found to work in lots of circumstances, but many organizations have their own styles for reports.

Obviously you should follow this specific guidance where you are doing an internal report, and you may like to do so as well for your Work-based assignment.

And you don't need to plan to write the report in the same order as it will eventually appear. Many people find that, having framed the aim, objectives and TORs, they can then select a title. Having done the research, the next thing to do is to prepare the main body of the report, so that conclusions and recommendations can be drafted. The summary follows, and often only then is the introduction written.

Activity 22

Work-based assignment

This Activity may provide the basis of appropriate evidence for your S/NVQ portfolio. If you are intending to take this course of action, it might be better to write your answers on separate sheets of paper.

You have your action plan and your subject for this report. Now it is time to select a title. Can you come up with something eye-catching and memorable as well as informative?

Have a look through the notes you made when you were thinking about what needs to be done. You may find inspiration there.

8 Manage the content

This isn't the place to discuss the ins and outs of logic, but your reports and your project won't succeed unless:

- your analysis and interpretation of data and other facts are correct;
- you present your arguments and ideas in a logical sequence;
- your conclusions are soundly based on your data.

It's a great deal easier to get this right if you did your preparatory work in the right order:

- thinking about the problem;
- considering your terms of reference;
- collecting your facts and figures;
- analysing the data;
- drawing your conclusions.

8.1 Keep an open mind

It may surprise you that I bother to tell you to draw your conclusions **after** you've collected your facts, but it's crucial. Plenty of people set out on projects and reports with their minds already made up. This causes all sorts of problems.

Take Wendy's report again. She set out with the conviction that something was wrong with the meals service. This is fair enough: she wouldn't have taken the trouble to produce the report otherwise. But she didn't begin with fixed ideas about precisely what should be done about it.

Activity 23 · 5 mins

Suppose Wendy has started from the conviction that the only solution was to 'contract out' the service to a commercial firm. What effects might this have had on her handling of the report?

_____

_____

_____

_____

_____

Now, we're talking about risks and tendencies here, not cast-iron certainties, but I would say that starting out with a strong attachment to a particular solution is dangerous because:

> 'Thus we have two options,' wrote Siobhan in concluding her report, 'to adopt a progressive policy of actively developing low-energy products for the future, or to remain committed to short-termism, stepping up the exploitation of the existing outmoded product range until we've wrung the last possible drop of profit out of a moribund market.'
>
> Well, it's clear which option she prefers!

- your mind tends to be closed to options other than the one you are set on;
- you may tend to overlook arguments and even evidence that support options that you don't favour;
- you will find it difficult to weigh up 'pro and con' arguments in a balanced way;
- you may find yourself using language and arguments in a manipulative way.

Those amount to bias, which often emerges when we pre-judge an issue. It's unconscious, for the most part, and is done in good faith, but all the same it's unprofessional and it distorts results.

Bias often also comes in when numbers are analysed and used. We shall look at this in detail in Session C.

9 Write your report

We have already seen that using emotive or manipulative language undermines the basic credibility of a report, but there are other problems with language too. When people get to the point of actually writing the report, they often have an attack of the most terrible pomposity, which makes the report unreadable.

9.1 Unreadable reports

Some situations (including the project report for the ILM Certificate in First Line Management) require a formal approach, i.e. writing in a passive rather than an active voice, or writing in the third person. Where this is not essential then bear in mind the following points.

a Try to avoid the use of management jargon, for example

'Exceptional competitive pressures experienced in the month of May are considered to account for the majority of the diminution in revenues deriving from overseas markets.'

Even if you understand it, surely it's much simpler for all concerned if you say:

'The fall in export sales in May is thought to be due mainly to unusually strong competition.'

> But ... writing style is a cultural issue. Most sensible people would much prefer something written in plain English, but there are some organizations and individuals who will object if you do.
>
> In that case, be realistic. Give them what they want: if you don't, you may reduce the chances of achieving your aims.

b   It is better generally to use active rather than passive language.

'Some 40 questionnaires were distributed' is passive;

It is more comfortable and straightforward to write:

'We handed out around 40 questionnaires'

c   Write in the first person.

'The author was inclined to dismiss this argument'

is better written as

'I was inclined to ...'.

Absolutely nothing is to be gained by writing in 'report talk'. Do what you would do in any situation where you want your written documents to communicate effectively:

■   write plainly, simply and directly;

■   keep it as short as reasonably possible.

9.2   Plain, simple and straightforward

Everyone will tell you to Keep It Short and Simple (KISS), but somehow few people manage to do so consistently.

This is what I recommend:

1   Write **Keep It Short and Simple** in big letters on a large piece of paper and pin it up where you can always see it.

2   When you come to edit your report give it a separate 'run-through' purely to simplify the language.

Activity 24 · 5 mins

Just to give you the idea, try cutting this passage down to size:

'Remembering the difficulties that were experienced when attempting to evaluate the effects of management changes on employee morale using non-parametric statistical analysis of questionnaire results, the author decided to eliminate this particular exercise from the survey, substituting instead a series of interview-style conversations in which the interviewer however diligently guided the discussion away from any tendency to digress or indulge in anecdotes.'

Phew! Write your version down here. My version can be found on page 118.

My version can be found on page 118.

EXTENSION 3
Several straightforward but comprehensive guides to grammar are available. They are non-academic, and give you plenty of examples and opportunities to practice. My choice is *Rediscover Grammar*, but in a large bookshop you may find other versions that you prefer. In the meantime, when you are sending out important letters on which a lot depends, get someone more experienced to check your final draft!

_____

_____

_____

_____

_____

_____

_____

_____

_____

You shouldn't necessarily expect to avoid all long words (there's nothing wrong with 'questionnaire' and 'digressing'). There may be no simple way of replacing a technical term like 'non-parametric statistics'. But in general, if there's a shorter and simpler way of saying something, go for it.

We deal with plain and simple writing in the workbook *Writing Effectively*. If you would like to go further into the subject of 'good' writing, including grammar and spelling, you may like to take up Extension 3.

10 Present your report

The first piece of advice on presenting your report is to examine a selection of reports that have been produced in and for your organization.

First the superficial view:

- How do they look? Which look more attractive than others?
- Which look most professional?

Then the practical considerations:

- Which look as though they'll be easiest to read and understand?

Activity 25

5 mins

Collect together some examples of reports. Take a good look at these reports. What can you learn from them?

_____

_____

_____

_____

First impressions count, whatever anyone may tell you.

10.1 Layout

Layout is about how you structure the page. It has a strong impact on both how the page looks, and how easy it is to read.

There are four golden rules for layout:

■ if in doubt, give it more space;
■ break up large blocks of text;
■ introduce some variety, for example by moving text in from the left hand margin (indenting);
■ use visuals (charts, diagrams, pictures) if you can.

You can afford to use a few sheets more paper.	You can't afford to make life difficult for the report's users.

Activity 26

5 mins

Look at the following layouts. Which of them would be most effective at getting the message across to the reader, and why?

The late Dr Mary Sheridan was a great expert on child psychology, but her written communications were more than a little testing. When she'd filled up a page in her scrawly handwriting, rather than begin another one, she'd start writing sideways up and round the margins, until the whole sheet was completely full of words going in all directions. Reading a page with no margins is horrible . . .

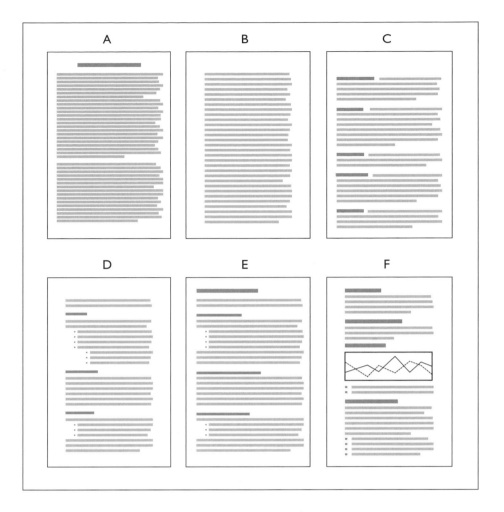

A The solid mass of words here is very off-putting: close spacing, narrow margins and long paragraphs will make reading it hard work.

B Double spacing and wider margins make this easier on the eye, but the monotonous block of text is still a problem.

C Better! Some headings at last, but what a pity there isn't space before and after the headings.

D A big improvement this time: good margins, headings with space around them, and indents to make points stand out.

E This is a step back compared with D, because of the narrower margins, but it's better than A, B or C.

F This one's excellent: margins, space, indents and – wonderful! – some graphics!

Activity 27 · 2 mins

Among those sample layouts, D and F are my favourites. But both of them lack three things that I consider essential in the page layout of a report or similar document.

See if you can identify the missing features.

_____

_____

_____

_____

My answer can be found on page 119.

In the end, how you lay out your report is up to you. You – and your readers – may have different tastes from me and mine. But, in case you can't make your mind up, here's how I would personally lay out the page as in F, with a running footer containing the page number, and the following margins: Left margin 5 cm, Top, right and bottom margins 2.5 cm.

10.2 Using a PC

Using a PC to produce your report will save a lot of time and effort.

This is true above all when it comes to making decisions about layout. The computer, with a word-processing programme such as Microsoft Word or WordPerfect, makes it extremely easy to adjust:

> There are plenty of books around that help you with designing and using templates in Word. Try _An Introduction to Word Processing Using Word 2000 or Office 2000_ if you use Word, or visit a big bookshop and browse.

- type size and style for text, headers and captions (which can all be different if you like);
- margins;
- the size and shape of diagrams;
- space around headings.

In fact you will be able to experiment, and to change the layout if you don't like your first version is quick and easy. You can even design a template so the process is automated, or you can use an existing template to save time. These are things that are extremely difficult if your report is handwritten.

However, if you have no option but to hand-write your report, here's a hint:

- work out the layout you want to use;
- take a sheet of A4 white card;
- rule the margins and line spaces strongly onto the card with a black felt pen;
- use this card as a template: the lines will show through the paper you're writing on and you will be able to produce regular, neat and consistent pages.

If you are preparing an ILM project report it should ideally be word-processed, though *neat* handwritten submissions are acceptable where this is unavoidable.

> You should now be ready to begin writing your report, if you have not already done so. Good luck!

10.3 Physical presentation

Finally, some common-sense ideas on how to present the report physically:

- print it on clean, quality paper;
- number all pages, including blank flysheets;
- make sure the contents page has correct page numbers for each section;
- fasten your report into a suitable folder or binder – a plastic wallet with a hard plastic spine, for instance, or a ring binder;
- make sure that your name and the date of the report appear prominently;
- keep a copy, even if this is only on disk, just in case the original gets lost.

Self-assessment 2

15 mins

1 a What word defines the broad purposes of a report or project?

_____

   b What word describes the specific things that you want to achieve?

_____

   c What phrase sets the limits and scope of the report and the investigations you will carry out?

_____

2 Put these stages of project preparation in the right order by putting a number 1–10 in the box:

   a setting TORs ☐
   b draft work plan ☐
   c writing first draft ☐

d producing final version ☐
e adding graphics ☐
f deciding aims and objectives ☐
g sorting and analysing your findings ☐
h thinking about the detail of investigations ☐
i carrying our your investigations ☐
j editing first draft ☐

3 Put these parts of a report structure in the right order by putting a number 1–9 in the boxes:

a title page ☐
b appendices ☐
c contents list ☐
d introduction ☐
e main body ☐
f recommendations ☐
g summary (including conclusions and recommendations) ☐
h conclusions ☐
i objectives/terms of reference. ☐

4 Put the following 'passive' sentences into 'active' form. Make any other improvements that occur to you

a Seven options were reviewed in total.

_____

b The findings of the consultants' report were not allowed to be revealed except to departmental managers.

_____

_____

c Appraisals must be countersigned by the appraisees themselves personally.

_____

_____

5 Which of these layout features will make a report easier to read and understand? (Tick as many as you wish.)
a Numbered paragraphs and sections ☐
b Keeping the writing short and simple ☐
c Using visuals ☐
d Keeping it short by getting as many words as possible on each page ☐
e Including lots of tables ☐
f Using indented text ☐
g Page numbers ☐

Answers to these questions can be found on page 116.

11 Summary

- If a project is going to achieve its objectives, it must be:

  - relevant;
  - thorough;
  - reliable;
  - credible;
  - readable.

- The report writing process involves:

  - focusing on the aim;
  - planning the work to be done;
  - researching and analysing the facts;
  - devising a coherent structure;
  - handling the content with logic and impartiality;
  - using language that is unbiased and simple;
  - presenting the report.

- Make sure you have all the items and space you need before you start work.

- You should start a project by clearly focusing on:

  - the subject;
  - the aim;
  - the specific objectives of the report;
  - your own specific objectives.

- Planning your work is crucial. It should include:

  - identifying the major stages in your work (this results in a time plan or schedule);
  - listing the key activities at each stage (which results in an action plan).

- A typical outline plan will include the following main stages:

  1 producing a rough workplan
  2 thinking about the detail of investigations
  3 carrying out investigations
  4 sorting, sifting and analysing your findings
  5 writing a first draft
  6 checking and revising
  7 refining the layout, adding visuals and so on
  8 producing the final version.

- The detailed action plan should work back from Day (or week) Zero, which is the deadline for submission. There should be extra 'float time' at points where difficulties may arise.

- Thinking is a key part of writing a report. You will need to concentrate, and to analyse data, ideas and arguments critically.

- The most important part of the report is the content of 'main body', in which the facts, arguments and ideas are presented.

- You should try to approach a report in an open-minded way. You should avoid using emotive, manipulative and pompous language.

- Keep focusing on TORs.

- KISS:

  - Keep
  - It
  - Short and
  - Simple

- The way a report is presented is important, because first impressions count. Page layout, smartness and a professional 'look' all count.

- In terms of layout I recommend:

  - using plenty of space;
  - breaking up blocks of text;
  - using indented text to introduce variety;
  - using visuals (charts, diagrams, pictures) if you can.

- Numbering of headings, sections and even paragraphs is expected in reports. It makes life easier for the reader, and for the writer too.

Session C
Gathering and presenting information

1 Introduction

When you write a report you are seeking to achieve certain personal aims, and also the aims of the report itself. But what you are primarily trying to do is to communicate.

We have already seen how planning, structure, logic, language and presentation all contribute to effective communication, but we have passed over the meat of the matter as it were:

- the research that needs to be done to obtain facts
- the analysis of the facts that needs to be done to generate information, conclusions and recommendations
- the presentation of the information.

So let us go back a little bit, to the point where you have finalized an action plan for how you are going to produce your report.

2 Obtaining facts

It is all very well knowing 'roughly' the sort of information that you might need, but another matter entirely to go out and find it.

Activity 28

6 mins

Cedric is a first line manager in a call centre. He has been asked to produce a report on how telephone costs could be minimized in his section. He has decided on his action plan for producing the report and knows what he has to find out about. For each item, suggest likely sources of information.

- the current provider and the services it offers;
- competitor providers and the services they offer;
- the volume of external calls made and received, their duration and timing;
- likely volume over the next two years;
- likely new services and clients over the next two years;
- alternatives to telephone calls.

_____

_____

_____

_____

_____

_____

Information will exist in the organization's own **record systems** about the current provider and the volume of calls. **External sources** such as directories, libraries, trade journals and the Internet could be used for information on competitor providers and alternatives to telephone calls. **People** inside the organization will be a useful source for information on what is likely over time. And Cedric can also conduct his **own investigations** to obtain information on all these topics.

2.1 Using record systems

Fortunately, as I've already said, most organizations produce large amounts of information – or rather, data.

Much of the data and information that you need will exist somewhere in the organization – the question, is where?

Here are some hints about getting the information that you will need.

Most information begins as unprocessed, bulk or 'raw' data. To make data useful, they have to be processed, analysed and presented in a digestible form. Information is data that have been made useful.

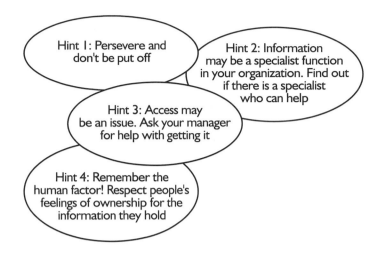

Hint 1: Persevere and don't be put off

Hint 2: Information may be a specialist function in your organization. Find out if there is a specialist who can help

Hint 3: Access may be an issue. Ask your manager for help with getting it

Hint 4: Remember the human factor! Respect people's feelings of ownership for the information they hold

Even if there's a sophisticated Management Information System in your organization, you may still need to rely on people to get at the data you need.

Activity 29 · 10 mins

Portfolio of evidence

S/NVQ D1.1

This Activity may provide the basis of appropriate evidence for your S/NVQ portfolio. If you are intending to take this course of action, it might be better to write your answers on separate sheets of paper.

Work-based assignment

Have a good think about what information you will need to acquire for your report, because you'll need to make plans to acquire it.

Use headings like these (you'll need at least one full sheet of paper).

- What information?
- Where is it?
- Whom do I need to talk to?

Highlight any of these that you think might present a special problem.

Consider what special steps you need to take to overcome these difficulties.

2.2 External sources

The great thing about **libraries** is that they tend to have librarians in them.

So, while it's extremely useful to learn how to find your way around a library yourself, you've got an expert helper on hand. In my experience, librarians and 'information service personnel' like nothing better than to help people like you and I dig out the sources we're looking for.

So especially where the information you need is in published reference works, technical manuals, official reports, research publications, directories or trade journals, the library's an excellent source.

But be warned: what you want may not be instantly available. It may take time to locate it, and it may be kept at a different site. Allow the library staff enough time to help you.

Another key source of course is the Internet or World Wide Web. You may even have an internal net, or intranet, in your organization; if you work in a sizeable organization, the chances are that someone else has also been looking for the same information.

By using a search engine and typing in a word or phrase relating to your research, you will be presented with a number of websites that offer information. By clicking on each one you can then go to the website and find out what you need to know.

There are some problems with the Internet: it doesn't have a librarian to guide and help you, and you may find that there is too much information available. Finally, it is unvalidated, i.e. 'cranky' information has the same chance of being accessed as information that has been properly researched.

So you need to be careful about information quality when researching on the Internet. What you don't have to worry about is being able to access the information, or having to wait for it.

2.3 People

We've already seen how people can help you find information, but people are also an important **source** of information.

Connor was working on an information booklet about the Research Institute for which he worked. The Institute was housed in a large Edwardian mansion in attractive grounds. Connor wanted to say something about the history of the house itself, before the Institute moved in, but no one seemed to know.

Eventually someone said 'Why not ask Mrs Olstead – her mother used to work for the family before the war'. Connor went to see Mrs Olstead and she was delighted to help.

Individuals who have been in the organization for a long time represent a kind of 'corporate memory-bank' which is a valuable resource. All too often this resource is neglected and under-used.

However, people are an important source of information in a different sense: they can be questioned about their ideas, knowledge, preferences, opinions. They can provide witness statements about incidents. Where your report involves examining how people feel about an issue, or how they behave in certain situations, you can go right out and ask them. In the next section we'll briefly consider how you can do so.

Activity 30

6 mins

S/NVQ D1.1

This Activity may provide the basis of appropriate evidence for your S/NVQ portfolio. If you are intending to take this course of action, it might be better to write your answers on separate sheets of paper.

Work-based assignment

Use this checklist to assess the quality of your evidence, and write brief notes to demonstrate how you have met these requirements.

- Where you've made a statement of fact, have you got the evidence to prove it?
- Are your data accurate and complete?
- Can you give references to show where the data came from?

If your answers suggest that you need to check or perhaps re-do some of your work, make plans to do this as soon as possible.

The last of our four main areas, your own 'investigations', may be more far-reaching and is something we will look at in the next section.

3 Conducting your own investigations

Your investigations will often involve talking to people:

■ informal discussions on the phone or face-to-face;
■ semi-formal interviews;
■ questionnaire-based surveys.

Don't treat these as an easy option. In order to extract maximum value from these encounters, you will need to:

■ plan your questions in advance;
■ listen carefully and take notes;
■ design your questionnaires with care.

3.1 How to listen

Most human communication takes the form not of talking, reading or writing, but of listening.

We listen in private conversations, on the phone, in meetings and in presentations, but the sad fact is we're pretty bad at it. We let our attention wander, we're in too much of a hurry, we don't take notes, and we don't ask questions.

Here are some hints for effective listening that you might find useful:

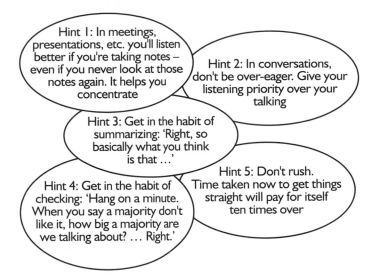

Hint 1: In meetings, presentations, etc. you'll listen better if you're taking notes – even if you never look at those notes again. It helps you concentrate

Hint 2: In conversations, don't be over-eager. Give your listening priority over your talking

Hint 3: Get in the habit of summarizing: 'Right, so basically what you think is that …'

Hint 4: Get in the habit of checking: 'Hang on a minute. When you say a majority don't like it, how big a majority are we talking about? … Right.'

Hint 5: Don't rush. Time taken now to get things straight will pay for itself ten times over

3.2 Questionnaires

Tina was told to report on team leaders' reactions to the 'adventure training' weekend they'd just been on. Since there were 15 people involved, she decided it would take too long to interview them all in person. Instead she drew up a questionnaire and sent it out in the internal mail.

Her questions included these:

1   Did you enjoy the weekend?

2   What did you think was best about it?

3   What did you think was the most useful part?

When Tina glanced through the responses, she realized she had a problem.

Activity 31

4 mins

Comment on the way Tina designed her questionnaire. Why do you think she had a problem with the responses?

_____

_____

_____

_____

_____

_____

_____

_____

_____

The problem with the questions is that although you can see what Tina's after, she won't get useful answers because of the way they're phrased.

Take Question 1 – Did you enjoy the weekend? Obviously, this begs the answer 'Yes' or 'No' (it is called a 'closed' question). What she needs to know is **how much** they enjoyed it. The way to discover this is to give people a scale on which they can reply, like this:

---

1 How much, on a scale of 1 to 10, did you enjoy the weekend

(1 = not all, 10 = immensely) ☐

---

or

---

1 How much did you enjoy the weekend (please tick one of the descriptions below)?

0   not at all   ☐
1   a little   ☐
2   moderately   ☐
3   quite a lot   ☐
4   immensely   ☐

This would enable Tina to **quantify** the results. She can simply add up the number attached to each response, work out what percentage that is of 48 (12 respondents times 4, which is the maximum possible score) and then quote the result as an 'approval rating'.

By contrast, questions 2 and 3 are much too 'open-ended', and all manner of replies are possible. Trying to quantify unstructured open-ended questions is a nightmare.

Instead Tina could have 'closed' them a bit, by listing the options she wanted people to choose from. Question 2 would then read:

---

2 What did you think was best about it? Tick **one** of the following:

The accommodation	☐
The meals	☐
The evening entertainment	☐
The group games	☐
The quiz etc...	☐

A sensible approach to making sure your questions are clear is to test them on a couple of people first. If you get answers you can't use, then you will have to rephrase the questions.

Two ways of using questionnaires

It's perfectly reasonable to send out questionnaires through the post (or by electronic mail). This saves time compared with talking to people direct, but there are drawbacks.

- Some responses will be late; others may never come back at all.
- There's no opportunity for the respondents to ask what your questions mean, or for you to clarify their replies.

An alternative, if the numbers aren't too large, is to use the questionnaire to conduct a 'structured interview'. Here you read the questions to the person, and write down their replies. This way you can get clear responses that you actually understand, and you can clear up any other issues while you're at it.

Once you have conducted your own research you are likely to have a lot of information. How do you get from this point to the point where you can form a conclusion?

The answer is by analysing the information, which is partly a question of sorting it into some sort of coherent order, and partly a question of analysing the numbers (the quantitative information).

4 Analysing numbers

EXTENSION 2
Most books on mathematics and statistics are academic in approach, and are not suitable for busy practical people. A notable exception is *The Effective Use of Statistics: a practical guide for managers*, a wide-ranging but fairly short book which contains a great deal of material that is relevant to your study of this workbook.

We don't have time or space to teach you 'number skills' in this workbook, but if you are going to do a lot of numerical analysis, you should be prepared to develop them.

I'll content myself with warning you about a few points to watch.

What's significant and what isn't?

I've already said a bit about this in Session A. Where you're comparing numbers, you'll always find small variations. These are inevitable, and they don't usually mean anything. Don't get trapped into worrying about small differences.

Big differences, on the other hand, need taking seriously. Where you come across something like the big variation in numbers of varicose vein operations described in Session A, you need to:

a consider the implications for revenue, staffing levels, workload, costs and profits;
b investigate the reasons.

Very well, you may say, but what is a big difference and what isn't?

A good question. And one that comes up all the time when we're analysing financial data such as sales, costs, and production figures.

Russ examined the monthly sales figures with great care. The company's policy was to consider de-stocking any item that fell substantially below budgeted sales levels, in order to make room for more profitable items.

Unfortunately there were more than 8500 different items on the monthly sales report printouts!

Here's a tiny sample of the printout:

Item code:	Units sold in month		Three-month cumulative	
	budget	actual	budget	actual
003687	515	498	1545	1466
003688	1644	1754	4932	5346
003689	201	155	603	412
003690	95	99	285	269
003691	779	702	2337	2010

Activity 32

8 mins

Russ has a major problem on his hands. How can he possibly make sensible judgements about which items are selling below the critical level, when he has to plough through 8500 items described in this way?

Think about this problem and make some suggestions about:

a what criteria could be used to decide which differences to query and which to ignore?

_____

_____

_____

b what extra information the computer could provide to make the task easier?

_____

_____

_____

It's about deciding when a difference is important enough to be worth investigating. Russ can't be expected to scan all these numbers visually and make sense of them. However, it would be possible to set down a 'criterion level' for each item. Then if the total was equal to or below this number, Russ could highlight it:

Item code:	Units sold in month		Criterion level
	budget	actual	
003687	515	498	465
003688	1644	1754	1521

However, this still leaves a mighty task, so we need to think about other options – perhaps using percentages instead of raw numbers:

Item code:	Units sold in month		Difference from budget	
	budget	actual	raw	%
003687	515	498	−17	−3.3
003688	1644	1754	+110	+6.7

Russ could then just scan the last column, looking for any figure more than, say, 10 per cent below budget.

The computer is of course perfectly capable of calculating these differences and percentages, providing that it is correctly programmed. Even better, from Russ's point of view, it can identify all those items that match the criterion 'sales more than 10 per cent below budget', and can print them out as a separate list. Bingo! No need to spend hours difference-spotting at all!

Computer spreadsheets are ideal for analysing numbers where you want to compare actual results with budgets or targets.

What this example shows is that you need to set levels at which you consider differences to be significant, and then if possible get the donkey work done by a computer.

Is it a trend?

One of the most useful things you can do with figures is identify trends. If you can show that:

- customer complaints are rising;
- sales of roofing materials are falling;
- discounts are increasing;
- the number of new inquiries is dropping

then you've found important information that may require urgent action – provided that:

- the changes are large enough to be significant;
- they aren't just random fluctuations.

What you are looking for are **significant** trends.

Activity 33 · 5 mins

Think about this table and the diagram based on it. What do they tell you?

| | Month sales £00s | | | | | | | | |
	1	2	3	4	5	6	7	8	9
Wood	522	672	528	510	555	631	509	561	616
Steel	1100	1261	944	1273	1134	1099	1215	1234	1311
Stone/sand	244	106	422	266	212	300	320	351	390
Total	1866	2039	1894	2049	1901	2030	2044	2146	2317

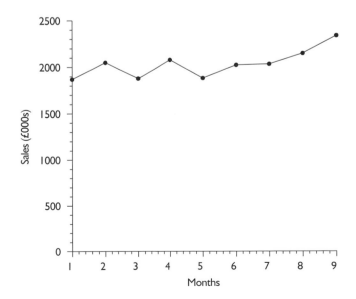

They seem to say that there's a rising trend. But look what happens when we add a further three months' data:

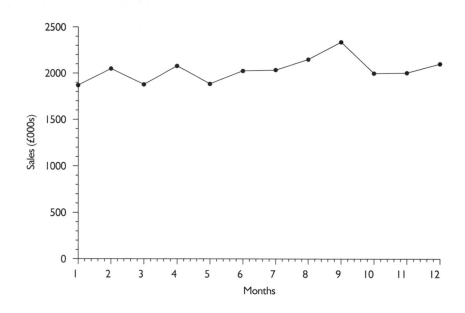

If there really was a trend before, it's gone. In fact it seems likely that these results are occurring at random within a range of about 1800 to about 2400, and that there wasn't even a temporary trend.

The only way to be sure is to add more data (and you can't necessarily wait for this) or to carry out much more sophisticated analysis. This, as I've already said, is beyond the scope of this workbook (see Extension 2).

5 Drawing conclusions and making recommendations

By this stage in the process you should be ready to reach some sort of conclusion based on your analysis of the information you have to hand. Obviously, I can't say what that conclusion will be, but you must make sure that it is:

- based on fact, not prejudice;
- backed up by valid evidence, the source of which you can state;
- logical.

Sometimes you can't resolve a problem or identify a solution – maybe all you can do is state the problem more clearly. This is still a conclusion. Often the conclusion of a report is: more research needs to be done!

Recommendations follow on logically from the conclusion, whatever that might be. They must be feasible, as far as you can tell.

6 Presenting information

Next time you watch the television news make a note of the different ways that figures are presented. It's very rare that the newscaster will just read out a list. You are much more likely to see a diagram or chart of some sort. These make it easier for us, the viewers, to take in information in a very short space of time.

How we present data can be as important as the figures themselves. So let's look at some useful ways of presenting data and information.

6.1 Pie-charts

We'll start with what are called pie-charts, taking a typical working situation.

Soonu is manager of a branch of a travel agency. She has just finished counting up some figures on sales of holidays for the last three months (January to March).

Head Office wants this information so that it can compare her branch with others. Soonu also wants to give her staff the same information. She writes a short memo to the National Sales Manager including a table of sales data. For the staff, however, she decides to add some graphics that she thinks will make the figures easier to understand.

76

Here is a diagram she has drawn to show how sales of holidays are distributed between destination countries.

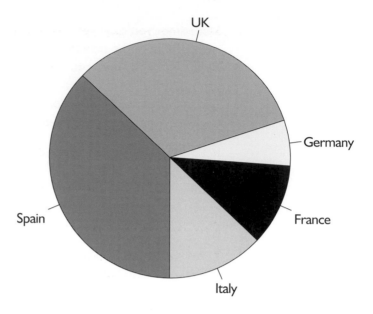

Diagrams like this are called pie-charts because they actually look like a pie which has been cut into different-sized slices.

Activity 34

5 mins

Look carefully at the pie-chart above and answer the following questions.

1   To which destination country have most holidays been sold?

_____

2   To which destination country have least holidays been sold?

_____

3   Roughly what proportion of holidays sold are to the UK as a destination.

_____

1 The largest slice of the pie is for Spain; however, there is very little difference between Spain and the UK, so you may well have thought they were much the same.

2 The fewest holidays sold were to Germany – the smallest slice of the pie.

3 About one-third of holidays are to the UK (Spain gets around the same proportion).

Advantages of pie-charts

■ they are easy to understand;
■ they make a strong impact, and catch the eye;
■ they make comparisons easy.

Disadvantages of pie-charts

■ we can't clearly distinguish smallish differences, such as those between Spain and the UK;
■ they don't tell us the actual numbers – for example, how many holidays were sold to the various destinations (though they could);
■ they can be confusing if there are many segments (slices), for example if many destination countries are shown.

So pie-charts are very useful for showing how a total is divided. They may be even more useful if we add the 'raw' figures, as Soonu could with the holidays, or the percentage of the share, as follows.

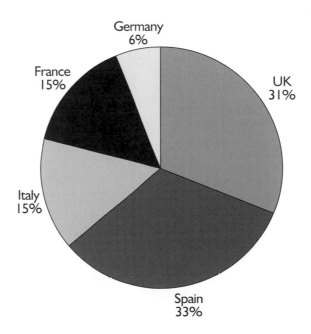

A pie-chart is useful when:

- we want to make an impact;
- the detail of the figures is not important;
- we want to draw attention to broad divisions in data.

We would not use a pie-chart when:

- we have a large number of divisions or groups;
- we want to draw attention to small differences between groups, because information cannot be seen clearly enough on the chart.

6.2 Bar-charts

Let's return to the travel agency example. In addition to the pie-chart, Soonu had drawn up a bar-chart for the number of holidays.

With a bar-chart the length of the bar shows the number of items in a category.

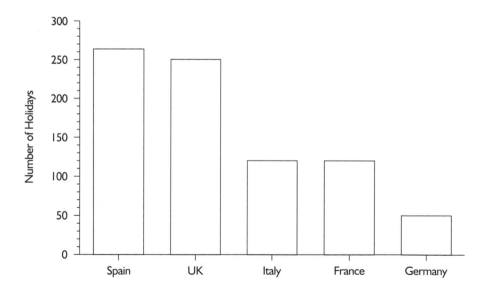

Note how the chart has been drawn. There is a separate bar for each country of destination which shows the number of holidays sold against the scale on the left. Thus we can see that the number of holidays sold for Spain is between 260 and 270, about 265. The number for the UK is slightly less, at 250.

Activity 35

2 mins

Approximately how many holidays were sold for

a Italy   _____

b France   _____

c Germany   _____

It's quite difficult to read precise figures off a bar chart, so we may not agree precisely, but the actual figures are 120 for Italy, 120 for France and 50 for Germany.

One of the things we are always trying to do with a diagram is 'make an impact' or 'catch the eye'. With bar-charts the impact can be increased by the use of colour. The bar-chart could be presented in one colour throughout or different colours for each country.

Sometimes the actual figures are shown just above the tops of the bars in vertical bar-charts. Alternatively, Soonu might have drawn her bar-chart horizontally, which would have made it easy to insert the figures.

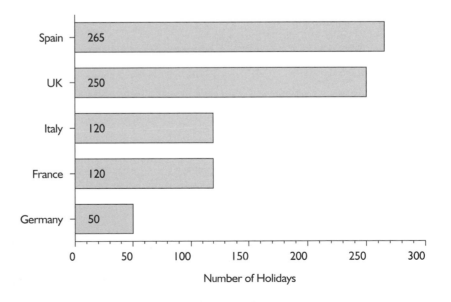

Number of Holidays

> One big advantage of a bar-chart is that it's usually easy to spot the highest and lowest values.

By shading the bars and adding the sales figures, she has improved the impact made by the chart.

By looking at the pie-chart we see the **share** of total sales of holidays to each country.

By looking at the bar-chart we can see **how many** holidays have been sold to each country. We can see clearly the difference between numbers of holidays sold to each country.

6.3 Tables

Soonu decided to show both diagrams to her staff, but only sent the bar-chart to Head Office, along with her memo and a table of figures. Here is the table she sent. Note that:

■ the headings are clearly identified
■ Soonu has used vertical lines to separate the columns of figures
■ she has boxed it in to make the table stand out.

Holiday sales (January to March)		
Country	**Number of holidays**	**Value of sales £000s**
Spain	265	53
UK	250	50.4
Italy	120	30
France	120	28
Germany	50	12
Totals	805	173.4

This is perhaps a slightly old-fashioned style: these days most people would not bother with the box and the vertical lines, though horizontal lines are almost always useful in tables where several figures appear on each line.

Note that word-processing programs such as Word can help you to produce excellent tables, but if you use a spreadsheet such as Excel it will generate the check for you as well!

Activity 36 · 2 mins

What information would the National Sales Manager be able to get from this table that he would not be able to get from the bar-chart that Soonu produced?

_____

_____

_____

_____

The table provides several extra things – the exact number of holidays booked for each destination, for example. Although we could include this on a bar-chart, we tend to pick up a broader, more general impression from a bar-chart. Similarly, the table shows the sales volume in money, which we could not show using the other approaches.

The one thing which a table makes clear, which the other diagrams do not, is **totals**. The table gives the total number of holidays and total sales value.

Tables, then, are useful, even essential, for showing detailed figures. But they lack the speed and impact of information given in diagrams, and have to be carefully examined before they reveal any useful information.

A pie-chart, bar-chart or pictogram (a chart that uses rows or bars of small images, instead of just lines) will instantly convey some information. Diagrams can also handle more complex sets of data. Two-directional bar-charts, for instance, can be helpful in highlighting movements of figures in opposite directions.

6.4 Graphs

Graphs are used almost everywhere when there is a need to record and display data that is recorded over time. Unlike bar-charts or pie-charts, graphs therefore represent two dimensions, and can be used to illustrate how things are changing. They can thus show much more information. For example, the sales breakdown figures in Soonu's pie-chart could be checked monthly and plotted on a graph to show the varying results for every month of the year.

This is what Soonu's firm did nationally to trace how sales progressed on a weekly basis. Here is a table showing sales of holidays to Spain from January to March.

Weekly holiday sales analysis: Destination Spain
January to March (weeks 1–13)

Week	1	2	3	4	5	6	7	8	9	10	11	12	13
Sales	44	39	28	34	24	14	19	16	10	12	8	10	7

Activity 37

5 mins

I have started to plot these figures on a graph. The vertical axis represents numbers of holidays, the horizontal axis represents weeks.

Complete the graph with figures for week 7 onwards.

Holiday sales January–March (weeks 1–13)

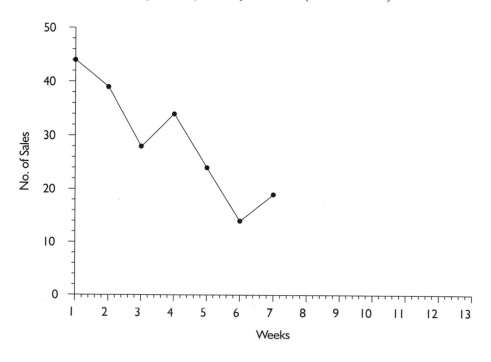

Now comment on what the graph reveals.

_____

_____

_____

To see how the graph should appear see page 119.

Once you've got the hang of using graphs it pays to practise this new skill. I produced the graphs and charts in this session using a computer spreadsheet, but graphs in particular are quite easy to draw up by hand. It is advisable to use graph paper.

Activity 38

20 mins

S/NVQ D1.1, D1.2

This Activity may provide the basis of appropriate evidence for your S/NVQ portfolio. If you are intending to take this course of action, it might be better to write your answers on separate sheets of paper.

You may well need to include data in your report, in which case you can use some of the ways of presenting them that you have learnt about here. However, it would be sensible to practise by creating at least two pie-charts and at least two graphs using other data first. If you look around you at work you will probably find plenty of data that it would be useful to turn into graphs or charts to help team members or managers appreciate the data better. These could also be included in your S/NVQ portfolio. When doing so you should include:

- the original data;
- the graph or chart you have made, with explanatory labels;
- a brief analysis of what the graph shows;
- a brief explanation of why this information is useful.

6.5 Comparisons using graphs

As I suggested earlier, more than one line of figures can be shown on a graph. Soonu's firm could for example show the pattern of sales to Spain and other destinations, all separately, on the same graph. This may get a little too complicated if there are more than about five lines, especially if they zigzag around a lot. Here we are comparing just two lines – Spanish and UK sales.

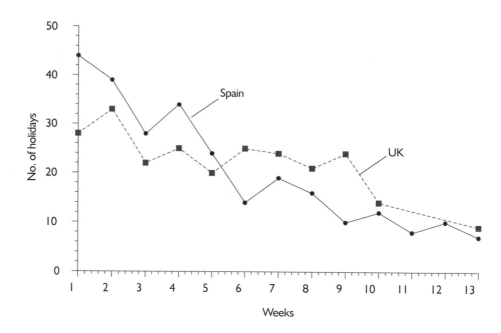

As you can see:

■ holidays to Spain sell better in the early weeks of the period
■ sales of holidays in the UK are more evenly spread over the period, but do start to fall away after week 9.

This information was available in accurate tables, but the graphic presentation reveals the changing pattern of sales at a glance.

7 Using appendices

We have seen throughout this workbook that data and information are vital to reports. How they are presented greatly increases the value of that report to its users.

But if you look at examples of completed reports you will see that, very often, there is very little numerical data in the report itself. Instead the writer will probably include appendices (singular: appendix) that contain all the data, leaving only a chart or graph in the main body of the report itself.

This is so that the user can choose whether to follow up the basic chart or graph with the more detailed numbers. If these are in the main body then the user has to work much harder, trying to separate the important bits of information from the 'back-up' data.

Deciding what should go where is one of the most important parts of presenting a report.

Activity 39 · 5 mins

S/NVQ D1.1

Work-based assignment

This Activity may provide the basis of appropriate evidence for your S/NVQ portfolio. If you are intending to take this course of action, it might be better to write your answers on separate sheets of paper.

Will you include the following in your report, and if so, where?

a   Terms of Reference

   YES/NO   Where? _____

b   definition of the problem

   YES/NO   Where? _____

c   background/circumstances/history

   YES/NO   Where? _____

d   assumptions/limitations/parameters

   YES/NO   Where? _____

e   definitions and explanations

   YES/NO   Where? _____

f   glossary of terms (if any)

   YES/NO   Where? _____

g   results of your investigation

   YES/NO   Where? _____

h   considerations of the impact of your proposals on costs and on people

   YES/NO   Where? _____

i   list of references (books, reports, articles etc. to which you have referred)

   YES/NO   Where? _____

I think that items f and i belong in appendices, while c, g and h clearly belong in the main body of the report. The remaining items should normally be in the introduction.

Self-assessment 3

15 mins

1 What are the four main sources of data for research?

2 What three ways can you think of to extract information from people?

3 Complete these statements about listening effectively.

  a You will find it easier to _____ on listening if you take _____

  b Give your _____ priority over your _____

  c Get in the habit of _____ what people have said and _____ what they mean.

4 You are designing a questionnaire to find out what customers think about your organization. How would you frame a question about:

  a how easy they find it to get through to the right person on the phone?

  _____

  _____

  _____

  b how often they buy goods and services over the phone?

  _____

  _____

  _____

5 What do we mean by a 'structured interview'?

  _____

  _____

  _____

6   Choose the correct word from the list below to complete this sentence:

When you select a manageable number of items for closer study your sample must be _____.

Choose from:

irrevocable
longitudinal
temporary
elastic
representative.

7   a   Here is a 'matrix' of features of three different types of chart. Write either YES or NO in each box to show whether the chart type has this feature.

Chart type	Features		
	Shows small differences clearly	Can show large number of divisions, groups or data points	Shows how things are changing over time
Pie-chart			
Bar-chart			
Graph			

b   One of the chart types should finish up with three 'NO's. What is it, and what **advantages** does it have?

_____

_____

_____

The answers can be found on pages 117–118.

8 Summary

- Some research and analysis is usually necessary – libraries, data record systems and people are important sources of information.

- If you set out to produce your own original data, take care:

  - make sure they are accurate;
  - check your calculations;
  - double-check your calculations;
  - make sure any questionnaires you use are properly framed.

- Listening and note-taking will also be important: make sure you use them effectively.

- Make sure that questions on questionnaires are not totally closed – unless you want simply 'yes' and 'no' answers. Equally, don't make them too open-ended. If you provide respondents with a list of possible answers and an invitation to rate their preferences, you will have quantified information as a result.

- Pay careful attention to the analysis of data. It's easy to:

  - misjudge the significance of small variances in figures;
  - identify 'trends' that are not really there.

- Use 'visuals' and graphics for greater impact and clearer explanation of key points and numbers. Pie-charts, bar-charts, graphs and diagrams are often used in reports, but you could also consider using plans, maps, photographs and illustrations.

Session D
Writing an ILM Certificate in First Line Management project report

This final session is primarily designed for those of you who are undertaking an ILM Certificate in First Line Management project. However, much of it is relevant for anyone who has to plan and write a report.

You will recognize most of the steps from the activities completed for your work-based assignment in Sessions A, B and C. Page references in the margins will point you back to the relevant sections, should you wish to review them. This session provides a more concise report-writing guide, drawing together all the steps into one list.

There is no self-assessment or summary in this session.

1 What an assessor looks for

The assessor will be looking for the following points in your project report (using the Assessment criteria continued in your copy of *Project Guidelines for Candidates*).

- Presentation

    - Is it well-presented and laid out?
    - Is there a useful table of contents, a summary (or graphics), an analysis of the current situation, details of the investigations, an evaluation of possible solutions and conclusions, recommendations, and appendices?
    - Is it likely to stimulate action?

■ Investigation

    ■ How was it researched and how much detail is included?
    ■ Are the facts supported by evidence?
    ■ How were problems overcome?
    ■ Are details presented in the main body and appendices, as appropriate?

■ Relevance

    ■ Does it focus on management, not just operational, issues?
    ■ Is all of the content relevant to your specific terms of reference?
    ■ Are alternative solutions generated and evaluated?
    ■ Does it meet the assessment criteria?

■ Completeness

    ■ Has adequate information been collected?
    ■ Have all aspects, including finance and human factors, been covered?
    ■ Is it roughly 2000–2200 words in length, plus appendices?

■ Information presentation

    ■ What charting, graphic and spreadsheet skills have been used?
    ■ Do they support the written text?

■ Conclusions and recommendations

    ■ Are they realistic?
    ■ Are they backed up by the information in the body of the report?

You should apply these checks yourself from time to time in the course of your work.

2 Choosing a project

See page 23.

Your project should deal with a **management** issue, not an **operational** one. It should not be large or complex, but must offer scope for improvement.

This means that it should:

■ address a **management problem** to which the solution is not clear in advance;
■ be geared to generating and evaluating **alternative solutions**;

- make use of **investigation**, not relying solely on the opinions of the writer;
- deal with the **human and financial** aspects of the issue, not the technical ones;
- focus on **evaluating** information, not just collecting facts.

You cannot simply 'write up' a recent event. You need to show that you can analyse a current situation, and make viable proposals to improve or move it forward for the benefit of the organization and the people in it. Think in particular about the management of productivity, profitability, customer service or working relationships, or reductions in waste, complaints, cost or labour turnover.

Examples of suitable topics for projects

- A critical survey with recommendations for improvement of:

  - current practice (staffing, recruitment, shift systems, rotas, etc.);
  - paperwork/people involved (for example, in the processing of orders from receipt to delivery);
  - the sales value of space in a retail business.

- An experimental piece of work:

  - a problem-solving exercise (to overcome a perceived difficulty);
  - a 'new-equipment' project (plant, machines, vehicles, apparatus);
  - a 'setting-up' project (new stores, canteen, social club);
  - a 'moving' project (efficient change of location).

- An investigation to find 'a better way':

  - improved layout of machinery or work-stations;
  - more efficient work-flow;
  - improved methods;
  - improved service to public/customer;
  - better recording/filing systems;
  - improved public relations;
  - improved communication between specific sections (e.g. sales and production).

- A feasibility study for:

  - new plant/equipment/facilities/premises;
  - new distribution pattern/area;
  - elimination of X;
  - addition of Y.

■ A 'what if' study, i.e. assessment of likely outcome of, e.g. centralization, decentralization or computerization.

■ A cost-saving exercise, i.e. more output with the same input, or the same output with less input.

■ A reorganization project of a section or department, of work allocation.

Action

■ Think about what project you are going to undertake.
■ Jot down half a dozen possibilities.
■ Against each, write a few words to sum up what you think will be the benefits, and the drawbacks of tackling this particular topic.

Benefits might include things like 'I'm doing this as part of my work already', or 'I'll learn a lot from this that will be useful to me later'.

Drawbacks might include comments such as 'will require a lot of travel', 'access to the information may be very difficult' or 'I don't have enough experience to tackle that one'.

3 Deciding aim and objectives

See page 36. The aim is a brief description of the overall purpose of the project.

Action

■ Write down your personal overall aim for the project in not more than 25 words

Objectives are the specific things that your report expected to achieve. They may be stated as part of the Terms of Reference (see D below).

Action

■ Note down your report's specific objectives.

4 Terms of reference

See page 19.

Terms of Reference (TORs) lay down the scope, parameters and purpose of your work, i.e. the areas the project is expected to cover, and those it is not.

ILM provide a generic set of Terms of Reference, and require that you use these as a framework for designing the specific TORs of your project:

1 to investigate the nature and scope of a management problem or situation within an organization in order to bring about an improvement

2 to generate and evaluate possible alternative solutions or ways to bring about the required improvement

3 to draw conclusions and make recommendations taking account of the **human** and **financial** implications

Action

■ Spend some time making sure that you can 'fit' your chosen project topic into this generic framework.

Agreeing terms of reference for your ILM project

The TORs are your authority to proceed, so your employer should agree the TORs of any work-based project. In bigger organizations, where many people have undertaken projects in the past, the training manager may hand you a piece of paper headed 'Terms of Reference'. This will probably contain a series of numbered paragraphs.

That's great, provided you are clear about what it is you have to do. (If not, try writing it down in your own words and then asking your immediate boss to check it out for you.)

Action

- Before you start your project you should submit the TORs to your ILM project tutor, who will confirm them with the External Verifier.
- Take careful note of any comments made by the project tutor and the ILM External Verifier.

5 An action plan for your project

See page 44.

The next stage is to work out an action plan or schedule. You may have to change it during the process of carrying out your investigation and writing it up but it is essential to have a plan in the first place.

Action

- Identify the major stages in your work.
- Estimate how long each will take.
- Draft out an action plan.

This can be simpler than those we discussed in Session B. In the example below we have included:

- just three columns: for date, week number (counting backwards from the deadline), and action;
- some 'float time': this is in case you meet unexpected delays.

Date	Week	Action
	15	select topic, prepare TORs
	14	clear with tutor and External Verifier
	13	plan content and coverage
	12	FLOAT TIME
	11	complete investigations
	10	start writing first draft
	9	FLOAT TIME
	8	create diagrams and other visuals
	7	revise and redraft
	6	submit to programme tutor
	5	FLOAT TIME
	4	FLOAT TIME
	3	final revisions; print out good copy
	2	recheck, edit and make corrections
	1	FLOAT TIME
	zero	submit final document

Remember, this is just an example, not a model. You may find you need longer in the earlier stages and less time for polishing up the final product. The important thing is to produce a realistic action plan which works for you. Having drafted your time chart roughly, produce a good copy and display it prominently. If you're using a computer, print it out. Ink in the dates and any other fixed points, such as the deadline.

Leave at least a week before your deadline.

You may be able to ink in some more items towards the end of the schedule. How long must you allow for the typing or word-processing of the final copy of your project report? I would allow at least a week. That puts 'Typing of final report' at zero minus two weeks, but building in a safety margin would make it zero minus three weeks.

Checking with your project tutor

Your ILM project tutor should read the final draft and may suggest some final amendments. Many calls are made on project tutors' time, so you should allow two weeks. And if posting rather than personal delivery and collection is involved, it would be wise to allow another week for that.

Working further back, you will need time for the final editing and tidying up – at least another week. We're now at something like zero minus seven weeks and we've not written a word!

Will it take you a month to write up? Or, with a buffer for safety, six weeks? If so, it's zero minus 13 for starting to write.

This means that all the fact-finding has to be completed 11 weeks before the deadline.

Action

■ Revise your time chart/action plan and draw up a final version.
■ Check it with your project tutor.

6 A structure for your project

See pages 16–21.

The structure is specified by ILM as follows. It is not identical to that in Session A, which you might encounter in any organization. In particular, it is almost certainly different to your own 'house style'.

1 Cover

2 Title page

3 Acknowledgements

4 Table of contents

5 Terms of reference

6 Summary (or synopsis)

7 Introduction

8 Main body of the report

- Present situation
- Investigation (or methodology)
- Evaluation of possible solutions

9 Conclusions

10 Recommendations

11 Appendices, cross-referenced

Ensure that you refer to the Project Specifications, which detail exactly what information is required in each section.

Checklist

The following should be included in your project:

a   terms of reference
b   definition of the problem
c   background/circumstances/history
d   assumptions/limitations/parameters
e   definitions and explanations
f   glossary of terms (if any)
g   description of the methods of investigation you used
h   considerations of the impact of your proposals on costs and on people

Action

See page 96.
■   Now look carefully again at the outline structure for the project provided by ILM.

7 Planning your investigations

See page 46.
Have a good think about what information you will need for your project, because you'll need to make plans to acquire it.

Remember to allow sufficient time for information gathering.

Action

■   List what information you need to acquire, where you expect to find it, and who you need to talk to.
■   Highlight any of these that you think might present a special problem.

You may prefer to set these items down in your time chart/action plan.

8 Reviewing the title

See page 17.

You probably have a working title.

Why not think the title through again? Can you come up with something that makes more impact? Something eye-catching and memorable as well as informative? You could get more flexibility by using a subtitle as well as the main title.

You may benefit from leaving the choice of a real title until last. It can often be restrictive to settle on a title this early. If so, leave the next action for now and come back to it later.

Action

■ Try thinking up a few possibilities on a separate piece of paper. Note down the best ideas.

9 A checklist for proceeding

■ Have you prepared a work-base for yourself?
■ Have you collected together the tools and equipment that you need?
■ Are you quite sure what your project is?
■ Do you know how widely you need to investigate and why?
■ Do you clearly understand what you have to do?
■ Are your TORs set down clearly?
■ Have the TORs been agreed with:

■ your employer (for a work-based project) or the 'validator' (for other types of project);
■ your project tutor and the ILM External Verifier?

■ Have you had your ideas session?
■ Have you identified the tasks you have to undertake and estimated how long you will need for each one?
■ Have you drawn up an action plan?
■ Are you organized and ready to start your project?

If that's all done, there's no reason to delay. Get started as soon as you can – and good luck!

10 Presenting the final version

You want your report to make a good impression to influence management and you know that it must therefore be well-presented. This means:

■ using professional language;
■ checking your grammar and spelling. The word processing package will help greatly here, but you should still check yourself – for instance, the package will tell you that 'form' is correct, even if you meant to write 'from';
■ word processing the report if at all possible;
■ numbering pages, and securing them in a binder;
■ using charts, etc. appropriately. Don't run out of time making them look beautiful – they are there for a purpose, which is to support your conclusion and recommendations;
■ putting as much information as possible in appendices;
■ ensuring that it has an appropriate title;
■ making a copy – you won't get your assessed one back.

As regards your conclusions and recommendations, try to avoid the following common errors:

■ failing to consider how changes you are discussing will affect people and the allocation of resources;
■ ignoring some non-quantifiable benefits, such as Health and Safety, improved communications and better motivation;
■ considering only the short term.

11 And finally – how Susan went about it

Susan Awalu is a hairdresser who completed her apprenticeship in London before moving with her family to Penchester, a busy Midlands city. She now works for an established and successful family business. For the last two years she has been their number one in the salon.

She is go-ahead, lively and keen to progress, so the firm decided that it was time for her to have some first line management training. They sponsored her for an ILM programme at the local college.

Susan is now involved in her project. The following details have been agreed between Susan herself, her employers and her ILM project tutor.

Title: The viability of a branch salon at Swanton

Terms of Reference:

1 To investigate the potential for a branch salon at Swanton.

2 To generate and evaluate possible locations and assess the initial and running costs of suitable premises, the cost of the equipment and the staffing required.

4 To draw a conclusion and make recommendations as to whether to proceed with the Swanton branch.

Susan was enthusiastic about this project and the possibilities within it for herself – she might become manageress. But she decided that hopes of promotion must not influence the investigations or bias her subsequent recommendations.

She carried out a thinking session, putting each idea onto a separate index card. She added fresh cards as additional thoughts occurred during the next few days.

About a week later she decided she had more than enough cards. It was difficult to juggle all the ideas. It was time to start consolidating her thinking. With some effort she managed to group together some of the single ideas under one heading. She then made out new cards for the headings, inserting additional comments as she went along.

The original number of cards had been reduced to a third and the file box was tidy and manageable. What was more, her own mind was tidy, having a clearer idea of what had to be done.

Susan's revised card file is set out on the next page. It is not in any particular order but it demonstrates that her thinking had covered a wide area.

While rewriting her cards she had noted possible who's and where's for gathering information. No doubt she would eventually realize that there would not be enough time to undertake all the areas of investigation she had thought of, but she set herself high standards, and that's no bad thing.

Action ·
20 mins

Consider Susan's cards. Give a priority rating (including noting those things that may have to be omitted). Now plan a time schedule on the blank form. Swanton is a market town some 15 km from Penchester. The firm will allow her time off and pay expenses to carry out investigations there on four separate days. Assume there are 26 weeks to **Deadline**.

PREMISES
'LOCK-UP TYPE'

GOOD LOCATION NEAR TOWN CENTRE
(AVOID HIGH COST PRECINCT)
CHECK LOCAL ESTATE AGENTS

NEED NOT BE AN EXISTING
HAIRDRESSING SALON

PREMISES
POSSIBLE PURCHASE
WITH A FLAT ABOVE? (S/C)
(INCOME FROM LETTING USEFUL)
SEE - ESTATE AGENTS · LOCAL PRESS
CHECK AGENT OLD ADS FOR INFO
FLAT? ME FIRST REFUSAL!!!
NB - SEE OBJECTIVE SUE

PLANNING
CHANGE OF USE? ANY SNAGS?
SEE TOWN PLANNING DEPT —
TALK OVER PROBLEM.

HOW TO MAKE AN APPLICATION.
WHAT COST INVOLVED?

DECORATIONS
(SHOP INTERIOR)

FIND SMALL DECORATOR
WHO KNOWS HIS JOB
PLUS — SIGNWRITER.
HOW TO WORK OUT A COST?
ALL Guestimated!!!

FIXTURES & FITTINGS
BASINS - PLUMBING - POWER SKTS
LIGHTING ETC. ETC. ETC.
(FOR BUILDERS SEE SHOP FIT LIST)
PLUS — HANDY ELECTRICIAN
FRIENDLY PLUMBER.
GUESSTIMATING LIKE MAD.

OVERHEADS GENERAL ?
RENT [IF A LOCK-UP]
RATES-WATER - PHONE
ELECTRICITY - (CHECK OLD
SHOP ACCOUNTS FOR FIGURES)
WOULD A CHANGE OF USE MEAN
RE-RATING PREMISES? LIKELY INCREASE
CHECK WITH RATING OFFICER

COMPETITION ???
CHECK OUT TOWN CENTRE
HOW MANY? CHECK THEIR
PRESENTATION STANDARDS -
CLEANLINESS. HOURS/DAYS OPEN
TYPE OF CLIENTELE? PRICES?
GAPS IN SERVICE OFFERED? !!!
BE DISCREET !!!

FLAT ABOVE SHOP?
IF LET - HOW?
FURNISHED? - UNFURNISHED?
GOING RATE IN TOWN?
CHECK LOCAL RAG.
ANY LEGAL SNAGS?
CHECK OUT WITH COLLEGE LAW
LECTURER (a Dishy number Jim)

— ADVERTISING —
CHECK WITH LOCAL WEEKLY RAG
COST OF ADVERTISING.
BIG SPLASH FOR OPENING DAY
REGULAR SPOTS
Don't tell them who you are
YET

SHOP STOCK
BASIC STOCK FOR SALON.
PLUS FOR RESALE TO CUSTOMERS
LIST PENCHESTER SHOP STOCK
COULD WE IMPROVE ON THIS?
CHECK TRADE JOURNALS FOR IDEAS
AND COSTS — SEE REF LIBRARY

NOTE TO SELF
WEEKS 14 & 15
SUNNING IT IN GREECE
By then I'll need sleep
more than sun

FUTURE POTENTIAL
IS THE TOWN STILL GROWING?
CHECK REF. LIBRARY + WEBSITE
FOR POPULATION BREAKDOWN
TOWN + 5 MILE AREA
ASK AT LOCAL PRESS ??

? → SUSAN AWALU ← ?

YOU ARE A NATURALLY
DISORGANISED ANIMAL ...
HAVE YOU THOUGHT
THROUGH ALL THE
ESSENTIALS ???

SHOP FITTING
(EXTERIOR)
IF CHANGE OF USE - COST OF REFIT?
IF EXISTING - COST OF REFIT?
CHECK 3 LOCAL BUILDERS
1 LARGE - 1 SMALL OUTFIT AND
TWO MEN & A DOG SET-UP.
NO QUOTES — JUST GUESSTIMATES

STAFF
LOCAL WAGES AS PENCHESTER?
PART TIMERS AVAILABLE?
TRAINEES?
[GOVERNMENT SCHEMES FOR 16
TO 18s - AND OTHERS]
CHECK WITH —
LOCAL JOBS CENTRE

— EQUIPMENT —
MAKE A LIST OF ALL EQUIPMENT
NEEDED TO START —
DRYERS-MIRRORS-CHAIRS -
TOWELS - OVERALLS ETC.
MAKE LIST OF PENCHESTER
EQUIPMENT ONE EVENING
? SECOND HAND BARGAINS IN TRADE PRESS

A MARKET SURVEY
BY S. AWALU & CO.
TAKE A DAY OFF (MARKET DAY?)
ASK WOMEN IF/WHERE THEY HAVE
HAIR DONE. WHY?
ARE THEY SATISFIED?
WOULD THEY LIKE SOMETHING EXTRA?
WHAT?? (I'D BE SCARED STIFF!)
COULD BE FUN

REPORT PREP NOTES
ALLOW 2 WEEKS FOR TUTOR TO
CHECK OVER BEFORE FINAL TYPING
ALLOW 1 WEEK TO AMEND AND
REWRITE. (HOPE NOT)
MUM WILL TYPE FINAL IN THE
EVENINGS: KNOWING MUM ALLOW
3 WEEKS AT LEAST

Date	Week no.	Things to be done

Performance checks

1 Quick quiz

Write down your answers to the questions below on *Project and Report Writing*.

Question 1 What one word completes this sentence correctly?

A report is a _____ of a large and complex area of information.

Question 2 Routine management reports have two purposes. The first is to show what happened – what we did, how much it cost, how much we earned, etc. What is the other purpose?

_____

_____

Question 3 These eight words sum up **four** key features of a good quality report. Arrange them into their correct pairs.

    argument
    clear
    consideration
    evidence
    logical
    presentation
    reliable
    thorough

_____

_____

_____

_____

Question 4   On top of those, what should a report always be, for the reader's benefit?

_____

Question 5   What is this a definition of?
A set of statements describing the focus and scope of a report.

_____

Question 6   When you are writing a report, there will be four main sources of information available to you. One is the organization's record systems. What are the other **three**?

_____

_____

Question 7   In questionnaires, interviews and surveys, what's the problem with asking 'open-ended' questions?

_____

_____

Question 8   What sort of things would you put in the Appendices to a report?

_____

_____

Question 9   'Those present were told by the security manager to remain seated.'

What's wrong with the way this statement is put?

_____

Question 10   KISS is a useful motto for writers. What does it stand for?

_____

Question 11   Complete this sentence:

One of the golden rules for laying out your report is 'If in doubt, give it more _____.'

Question 12   You want to use a graphic to show how last year's sales of three products compare with this year's. Would you use a pie-chart, a bar-chart or a graph?

_____

Question 13   Visuals, diagrams and graphics work because visual communication is more effective than written or spoken communication. What is the other good reason for using them?

_____

Answers to these questions can be found on pages 120–121.

2 Workbook assessment and Work-based assignment

You will already be familiar with the combined Workbook assessment and Work-based assignment for this workbook introduced to you in Session A and developed through Activities 11, 17, 20, 21, 22, 29, 30 and 39.

Reflect and review

1 Reflect and review

Now that you have completed your work on *Project and Report Writing*, let us review our workbook objectives.

■ When you have completed this workbook you will be better able to identify what a report is about and who it is for.

In the first session of this workbook we have concentrated on the aim of a report, its objectives and the objectives of its writer (which aren't the same thing), and the needs of the report's users. All these must be clear before work commences. If the report has no coherent aim then you can't realistically set about all the work involved in producing one. If you don't have a clear objective – such as 'getting a useful report completed on time', rather than 'getting my manager off my back', you will not be positively motivated enough to do a good report. And if it is not clear whether the report is routine or special, for decision making or persuasion, then it will be very difficult to plan and structure the investigations properly.

■ What do you think are the most important aspects of the user's needs that you should consider?

_____

_____

_____

- When you have completed this workbook you will be better able to plan and prepare for writing a report;
- to identify and collect the relevant data and information;
- to analyse and interpret data correctly.

Reports have a very important function, especially in management. They are used to summarize and pre-digest complex information for the benefit of decision makers. It's vital that they should be thorough, accurate and reliable, and this means taking pains over the planning and preparation of the report. This is particularly true of special 'one-off' reports and ILM Certificate in First Line Management projects.

Now you have completed your reading and responded to the activities, you should have a much clearer idea of how to plan and prepare for writing a report.

- Which of the aspects of planning and preparation that you have learned about are likely to be most useful to you?

_____

_____

_____

Reports are based on information, so obviously the collection and analysis of that information is crucial to the quality and usefulness of the report. Remember the case study of Jamail's report about improvements to council premises in Session B. Jamail didn't bother to 'do his homework', and the upshot was a 'report' that was completely useless for practical purposes.

- Having worked through the activities relating to collecting and analysing information, what particular points will you make sure to check when you next write a report?

_____

_____

_____

Among the other objectives was this one:

■ When you have completed this workbook you will be better able to adopt a suitable structure for your report.

Structure, as we explained in Session A, is important for two reasons: it helps the writer organize the document, and it helps the reader understand it. Report structures can vary, according to the subject and the purpose. Some will contain separate summaries, appendices or recommendations, while others will not. Broadly speaking, however, all reports follow the same pattern – a beginning, containing the title, summary, contents list, and any necessary explanations; a middle (the 'main body'); and an end. This contains the conclusions and so on.

■ How would you adapt your structure for particular kinds of reports? What elements should always be there?

_____

_____

_____

The next two objectives deal with the way you write and present your reports.

■ When you have completed this workbook you will be better able to write clearly and simply and present your arguments in a fair and unbiased way; and use tables, diagrams and graphics effectively.

The goal must of course be to make sure your report communicates effectively. Take care over your use of language – the words, phrases and sentences with which you express the facts and ideas contained in the report. The more simply and clearly you write, the better you will communicate, and with few exceptions, it also pays to adopt a friendly and 'personal' style.

■ Since studying this workbook, what improvements have you started to make to the way you write?

_____

_____

_____

_____

On a more technical level, both the physical layout of your report and the way you use tables and graphics have a strong impact on readability. As we explained in Session C, visual means of communication often work better than words, but all kinds of 'extra' material have an additional benefit too. By breaking up solid walls of text they make the reader's task noticeably easier. Anything you can do to help the reader will help you communicate.

■ What will you now be doing to make your documents easier work for the reader?

_____

_____

_____

We used what we learned in the first part of the session to feed into the practical objectives.

■ When you have completed this workbook you will be better able to plan and produce an ILM Certificate in First Line Management report.

The Certificate report is a major part of the assessment for the Certificate, and a very important part of your personal development as a manager. It gives you practical experience in identifying and solving problems, lets you apply your skills and knowledge in the workplace, helps with developing your communication skills, and offers the chance to make a real contribution to your own organization's effectiveness.

■ What do you think you will gain most of all from your work on the ILM Certificate in First Line Management project?

_____

_____

_____

Finally, can you now be confident that you will be able to achieve our last, and most important objective – **to produce a report that is thorough, reliable, credible and readable?**

2 Extensions

Extension 1

Ways of researching

There are many ways to conduct research.

■ Observation

Using your eyes and noting what is seen.

■ Experiment

This could be a 'laboratory-type' experiment or it could be trying something out, such as a method, a system, a machine, sometimes a series of trial runs. Careful notes and records are kept of what is tried and of the results.

■ Measuring

Counting, weighing, using a ruler or tape measure, skilled assessment. All recorded for subsequent comparison/evaluation.

■ Collection

Gathering together information on one subject from different sources. For example, from suppliers, users, customers, experts, people close to the information, old files, current files, libraries. Information may be requested by letter, memo, phone, e-mail, face-to-face talking.

■ Selection

Selecting information from one or several sources: for example, picking out relevant figures from computer print-outs.

■ Sampling

Investigating a random selection of a larger total number of items to gather specific data. The aim is to collect data which is representative of the whole.

■ Interviewing

Getting information from people by asking them questions face to face. This may be a matter of making an appointment with one individual with specialized knowledge. Or it could be a matter of interviewing several in order to get opinions. In the latter case it is advisable to prepare a list of questions beforehand for the sake of consistency.

■ Questionnaire

Getting information from people by asking them to indicate answers to questions set out on paper.

Extension 2

Book	*The Effective Use of Statistics: A Practical Guide for Managers*
Author	Tim Hannagan
Edition	Second Edition 1999
Publisher	Kogan Page in association with Chartered Institute of Management Accountants

A user-friendly guide designed to help you cope with numerical data even for those with limited mathematical knowledge. The book provides the essential statistical grounding to handle, interpret and communicate the information to others. It provides numerous examples and case studies and comes with a disk containing worksheets and relevant data to help you collect, analyse, present and forecast from statistical information.

Extension 3

Book	*Rediscover Grammar*
Author	D Crystal
Edition	1988
Publisher	Longman

The book goes into great depth in explaining the rules of English grammar and its complexities in a clear and concise format that makes it easy to understand. Ideal for anybody who is having difficulties with English grammar or anybody who simply wants to correct the grammar that they use in day-to-day life.

Extension 4

Book   *An Introduction to Word Processing using Word 2000 or Office 2000*
Author   Fiona Watt
Edition   2000
Publisher   Usborne Publishing Ltd

This is just one of many books on the market which offer guidance to the beginner on how to use the most common word processing packages to produce good quality material. To find one that suits you and your computer's setup, try visiting a big bookshop and browsing through the many titles on offer.

3 Answers to self-assessment questions

Self-assessment 1 on page 24

1   These statements should read:

    a   A report examines an area of information and **summarizes** all the important issues.
    b   Many routine reports are designed to reveal significant variations.
    c   The role of a management report is to pre-**digest** information for **decision**-makers.
    d   A report, to be useful, should feature:

       ■ clear **presentation**;
       ■ thorough **consideration** of the issues;
       ■ reliable **evidence**;
       ■ **logical** argument.

2   Regular, routine reports are fairly straightforward to produce because they're produced in a standard format, on a regular basis, and both the writers and the readers become thoroughly familiar with them.

3   Examples of the kind of reports that might be needed 'for the record' include anything that might involve:

       ■ a legal issue;
       ■ an insurance claim;
       ■ serious incident of some kind;
       ■ an accident;
       ■ events leading up to a serious disciplinary issue.

4   relevant, thorough, reliable, credible and readable.

5 Title page; contents list; objectives/terms of reference; summary; introduction; main body; conclusions; recommendations; appendices.

Self-assessment 2 on page 58

1 a The word that defines the broad purposes of a report or project is **aim**.
   b The word that describes the specific things that you want to achieve is **objectives**.
   c The phrase that sets the limits and scope of the report and the investigations you will carry out is **terms of reference**.

2 Put these stages of project preparation in the right order:

f deciding aims and objectives	1
a setting TORs	2
b draft work plan	3
h thinking about the detail of the investigation	4
i carrying out your investigations	5
g sorting and analysing your findings	6
c writing first draft	7
j editing first draft	8
e adding graphics	9
d producing final version	10

3 These are the parts of the structure in the right order:

a title page	1
c contents list (this will be written last)	2
i objectives/terms of reference	3
g summary (including conclusions and recommendations)	4
d introduction	5
e main body	6
h conclusions	7
f recommendations	8
b appendices	9

4 I would re-write these three sentences as follows:

   a Altogether we (or perhaps they) reviewed seven options.
   b Only departmental managers may see the consultants' findings.
   c Appraisees must countersign their appraisals.

5 All of these will help make a report easier to read and understand except d and e.

   d is completely the reverse of what's needed. You should use generous margins and plenty of 'white space'.

   Including a few short tables is fine, but (e) is counter-productive.

Self-assessment 3 on page 86

1   The four main sources of data are internal record systems, external sources, people, your own research.

2   You can extract information from people by means of informal discussions, semi-structured interviews and questionnaire-based surveys.

3   The statements about listening effectively should read as follows:

   a   You will find it easier to **concentrate** on listening if you take **notes**.
   b   Give your **listening** priority over your **talking**.
   c   Get in the habit of **summarizing** what people have said and **checking** what they mean.

4   a   A question about how easy it is to get through to the right person on the phone should be something like this:

   When you ring us, how easy is it to get through to the person you need to speak to? (Please tick one box.)

   very difficult ☐
   quite difficult ☐
   not a particular problem ☐
   quite easy ☐
   very easy ☐

   b   A question about how often they buy goods and services over the phone should be phrased something like this:

   How many times a year do you buy goods over the phone?

   never ☐
   1–3 times ☐
   4–6 times ☐
   7–10 times ☐
   more than 10 times ☐

5   A 'structured interview' is one in which you work through a series of prepared questions and note down the answers at the time. You can often use a questionnaire in this way.

6   When you select a manageable number of items for closer study your sample must be **representative**.

7 a Your matrix should look like this:

| | Features | | |
Chart type	Shows small differences clearly	Can show large number of divisions, groups or data points	Shows how things are changing over time
Pie-chart	NO	NO	NO
Bar-chart	YES	YES	NO
Graph	YES	YES	YES

b The pie-chart gets three NOs. However, pie-charts have three advantages:

- they are easy to understand;
- they make a strong impact, and catch the eye;
- they make comparisons easy.

4 Answers to activities

**Activity 24
on page 53**

Note that the writer uses long words, long phrases, and that the whole thing (63 words) is one long sentence.

> I had problems using non-parametric statistics to analyse the questionnaire about how management changes affected morale, so I decided to abandon this approach. Instead I did a series of interviews in which I carefully steered people away from digressing and from personal stories.

That's 43 words, and a lot clearer, I think.

Activity 27 on page 56

The three features that are missing are:

- page numbers, which are essential;
- a 'running header' or 'running footer' (a line of text at the top and bottom of each page that contains the title of the report and perhaps details like date of submission and the writer's name);
- numbering for the headings and sections. Numbering is a must: it helps you organize the report, and it **greatly** helps other people read, consider and discuss it. It's so much easier (and safer) to say 'In paragraph 3.1 on page 16, what do you mean by ...?' than to try to refer to a passage in unnumbered sections.

Activity 37 on page 82

Here is the completed graph. It clearly shows a steady fall over the period covered.

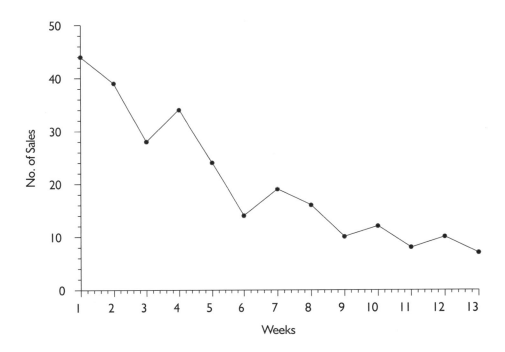

The advantages of the graph over the table are that:

- it creates a good visual impact;
- it immediately shows how sales have been moving;
- it emphasizes the downward movement of the sales data.

5 Answers to the quick quiz

Answer 1   A report is a **summary** of a large and complex area of information.

Answer 2   The other purpose of routine management reports is to **reveal** significant variations.

Answer 3   The four correct pairings are:

clear presentation
thorough consideration
reliable evidence
logical argument

Answer 4   A report should always be **readable**.

Answer 5   A set of statements describing the focus and scope of a report is called the **terms of reference**.

Answer 6   When you are writing a report, there will be four main sources of information available to you: the organization's record systems, libraries, people and your own investigations.

Answer 7   The problem with asking 'open-ended' questions is that the answers are so varied that they're difficult to analyse and quantify.

Answer 8   The Appendices of a report are a useful place to put background, technical and supporting material, which the reader may like to consult, but doesn't necessarily want to read in detail.

Answer 9   This statement unnecessarily uses the 'passive voice'. It would be better to say: 'The security manager told those present to remain seated.'

Answer 10   KISS stands for **keep it short and simple**.

Answer 11   The sentence should read:

One of the golden rules for laying out your report is: 'If in doubt, give it more **space**.'

Answer 12   The best choice is a bar-chart, in which you would place the two years' figures side by side.

Answer 13   The other good reason for using visuals, diagrams and graphics is that they bring variety into the report.

6 Certificate

Completion of this certificate by an authorized person shows that you have worked through all the parts of this workbook and satisfactorily completed the assessments. The certificate provides a record of what you have done that may be used for exemptions or as evidence of prior learning against other nationally certificated qualifications.

Pergamon Flexible Learning and ILM are always keen to refine and improve their products. One of the key sources of information to help this process are people who have just used the product. If you have any information or views, good or bad, please pass these on.

INSTITUTE OF LEADERSHIP & MANAGEMENT

SUPERSERIES

Project and Report Writing

....

has satisfactorily completed this workbook

Name of signatory ....

Position ....

Signature ....

Date ....

Official stamp

Fourth Edition

INSTITUTE OF LEADERSHIP & MANAGEMENT
SUPERSERIES
FOURTH EDITION

Achieving Quality	0 7506 5874 6
Appraising Performance	0 7506 5838 X
Becoming More Effective	0 7506 5887 8
Budgeting for Better Performance	0 7506 5880 0
Caring for the Customer	0 7506 5840 1
Collecting Information	0 7506 5888 6
Commitment to Equality	0 7506 5893 2
Controlling Costs	0 7506 5842 8
Controlling Physical Resources	0 7506 5886 X
Delegating Effectively	0 7506 5816 9
Delivering Training	0 7506 5870 3
Effective Meetings at Work	0 7506 5882 7
Improving Efficiency	0 7506 5871 1
Information in Management	0 7506 5890 8
Leading Your Team	0 7506 5839 8
Making a Financial Case	0 7506 5892 4
Making Communication Work	0 7506 5875 4
Managing Change	0 7506 5879 7
Managing Lawfully – Health, Safety and Environment	0 7506 5841 X
Managing Lawfully – People and Employment	0 7506 5853 3
Managing Relationships at Work	0 7506 5891 6
Managing Time	0 7506 5877 0
Managing Tough Times	0 7506 5817 7
Marketing and Selling	0 7506 5837 1
Motivating People	0 7506 5836 3
Networking and Sharing Information	0 7506 5885 1
Organizational Culture and Context	0 7506 5884 3
Organizational Environment	0 7506 5889 4
Planning and Controlling Work	0 7506 5813 4
Planning Training and Development	0 7506 5860 6
Preventing Accidents	0 7506 5835 5
Project and Report Writing	0 7506 5876 2
Securing the Right People	0 7506 5822 3
Solving Problems	0 7506 5818 5
Storing and Retrieving Information	0 7506 5894 0
Understanding Change	0 7506 5878 9
Understanding Finance	0 7506 5815 0
Understanding Quality	0 7506 5881 9
Working In Teams	0 7506 5814 2
Writing Effectively	0 7506 5883 5

To order – phone us direct for prices and availability details
(please quote ISBNs when ordering) on 01865 888190